GW01311246

Mourn

the

Beloved Country

by

CHRISTOPHER R CORNISH

Christopher R Cornish

Copyright © 2021 Christopher R Cornish

All rights reserved.

DEDICATION

This book is dedicated with love to my wife and our five beautiful daughters.

TABLE OF CONTENTS

ACKNOWLEDGMENTS

I wish to acknowledge and express my appreciation to the following without whose help and support the long road to publication of this book would have proved much more difficult:

my loving wife, Denise for her love and encouragement; my friend, David Price for his kind assistance and many hours spent on editing; my publisher Work4u247 Ltd; Kin Bentley for the Foreword; Scott Balson for his comprehensive Review and support; and, all my family and friends. Individual acknowledgments are also made in the book.

FOREWORD TO "MOURN THE BELOVED COUNTRY"
By KIN BENTLEY

Western nations colonised much of the world over several centuries, culminating in the "Scramble for Africa" between 1881 and 1914.

The major difference between South Africa and particularly the other British colonies is that initially there was no intention of establishing a substantial settlement at the Cape, merely a replenishment station for ships sailing to the East.

Secondly, there was never any large, ongoing plantation of European settlers in South Africa.

Furthermore, once the few million Europeans established wealth-creating industries and substantial commercial agricultural enterprises in the 19th century, South Africa was confronted with the prospect of a never-ending influx of migrants from the north. This was over and above the indigenous people of the region, who already substantially outnumbered them.

Whites may have held political power, but demographics would ultimately decide matters. That much was always clear, however one tried to square the circle.

Even before the African National Congress opened the floodgates after 1994 through lax border control people had flocked from countries to the north to look for work on the diamond, gold and other mines opened up by mainly British entrepreneurs, exemplified by Cecil John Rhodes.

But there was only ever a half-hearted approach to the colonisation of South Africa, unlike with the other currently far more affluent colonies of the British Commonwealth, where small indigenous populations were dealt with ruthlessly and totally overwhelmed. That was never going to happen to the same degree in South Africa, at the foot of the massive African continent.

After the Dutch East India Company set up a small fort and farm at the foot of Table Mountain in 1652, it took the Dutch "Trekboers" more than 100 years to incrementally occupy the territory between Cape Town and the Fish River in the east, a distance of about 1,000km. This was a sparsely populated area, with the Dutch Africans on their massive stock farms eventually becoming primarily pastoralists like the westward-migrating Xhosa, whom they met and came into conflict with on the eastern border of the Cape Colony towards the end of the 18th century.

It was here, in the Albany district, that Britain helped fund the only major plantation of its citizens in South Africa, when some 4,000 settlers sailed out from British ports from late 1819 and by mid-1820 had been placed on farms in the Suurveld, an area unsuited to the sort of agriculture that their small "locations" were meant to sustain. Ultimately, the true aim of Lord Charles Somerset, the Cape Governor, was to use these settlers as a buffer between the Xhosas to the east and the colony.

Four thousand British settlers ensured that English became the lingua franca, especially in the Eastern Cape, where they outnumbered the Dutch/Afrikaners. Indeed, this change from distant DEIC rule to more intrusive British imperial rule led to thousands of Afrikaners loading up their ox-wagons and trekking into the hinterland from 1836, where they established republics in the Orange Free State and Transvaal.

The English language and culture spread as the British settlers moved around the sub-continent, opening up new ports like Durban and East London, and trading with the indigenous tribes, while missionaries spread literacy among this Iron Age population.

But those 4,000 settlers could and perhaps should have been four million, which would have changed the complexion of the colony completely. Because during the 19th century, no fewer than 25 million souls emigrated from the British Isles. The United States, Canada, Australia and New Zealand were the main recipients of this

iii

injection of expertise and cultural evolution. The flow of European emigrants to South Africa was a trickle by comparison.

Chris Cornish was a relative newcomer, arriving in South Africa as a young child in the early 1950s. But he grew up here and as a result became an English-speaking South African. He worked hard, trained as a lawyer and conveyancer, and, with a large family of five daughters, enjoyed a good life, albeit that the shadow of the above-mentioned impending demographic disaster hung increasingly over everyone as the decades passed.

Handing political power to the ANC in 1994 seemed like a solution. But, as I have written in my own autobiography, the non-racial rainbow nation that Nelson Mandela and Desmond Tutu promised never materialised.

Chris outlines in detail, all too familiar to those of us who keep abreast of the news, how things have gone from bad to worse under the ANC. Its racist Black Economic Empowerment and Employment Equity laws, along with systemic affirmative action based on an eight-to-one ratio of black-to-white representivity in state-owned enterprises, government departments, municipalities and increasingly the private sector, has steadily eroded an economy that was once the pride and envy of Africa.

One cannot blame those like Chris, retired and with age-related illness a growing concern, for wanting to get out of this jam before South Africa really hits the skids, as Zimbabwe did just over 20 years ago when Robert Mugabe seized 4,000 white-owned commercial farms. This catastrophic move, which decimated the economy, was endorsed by then South African president Thabo Mbeki and the ANC in general. It set the tone for the steady destruction of South Africa itself, as Zimbabwe was seen as having set a good example for us to follow.

South Africans of European descent have long lived on a knife-edge, never knowing when it would be best to try to flee the sinking ship. Some are fortunate to have dual citizenship and are able to emigrate to better-run countries where they aren't discriminated against on the basis of their race; at least not yet. But most whites, especially those with adult children who have retired or are close to doing so, are not that fortunate. And even if they were, their savings and pensions would usually be almost worthless in first-world currencies. The rand, on a par with the dollar in the 1960s, now hovers around R14 to the greenback. It has gone from R2 to the pound sterling in 1961 to around R20 today.

This story is tragic in so many ways. Instead of seeing out your golden years in a country you helped build through decades of paying taxes in a peaceful, well-run environment, you are faced with failing water and electricity supplies, potholed roads, dysfunctional municipalities and rampant corruption within all levels of government.

Many have children who have emigrated in the face of affirmative action laws which have prevented them from advancing along their chosen career paths.

The legacy of 27 wasted years of ANC mismanagement is the steady decay of once-beautiful cities, which are now increasingly surrounded and invaded by shanty towns like you get across Africa. A vicious circle has emerged of a stagnant economy and too many unemployed and unskilled people, poor state schooling and once-proud universities that have become havens for state-sponsored racists affiliated to the extremist Economic Freedom Fighters.

Chris Cornish is right to title his book Mourn the Beloved Country. Few sane, sensible people mourned the ending of apartheid, which was a reprehensible system. But almost everyone is now mourning the loss of a country through a process of systemic racial preferencing, corruption and maladministration.

Is there light at the end of the tunnel? For the "Remainers" all we can do is hope.

This is the southern end of Africa, after all.

Kin Bentley

Port Elizabeth

2021

After studying fine art for four years and an initial two years of military conscription, Kin Bentley worked in East London as an organiser for the liberal Progressive Federal Party from 1981 till 1984. For the next 32 years he worked as a reporter and then as a sub-editor on the Port Elizabeth newspapers, the Evening Post and the Eastern Province Herald. This included two years, 1990 and 1991, as London correspondent for SA Morning Newspapers. Since his retirement in 2016 he has published his autobiography, After the Storm and Before the Rainbow (Footprint Press, 2019) and 200 Years, A Celebration of Port Elizabeth (GFI, 2020).

Review by Scott Balson, Presenter at lovinglifetv.com – an influencer with a massive following, as an observer and reporter on the South African Political Arena:

I feel like Chris and I are cut from the same cloth. Much of his experiences of life in and around Africa reflect mine. Chris is a few years older than me but sailed on the Edinburgh Castle back in the early 1960s - as I did. That is how colonial families travelled to and from Africa back to England in those days. My fondest memory of this time was crossing the Equator and watching the Captain of the ship unilaterally rule on invented crimes of passengers who were dunked in the pool or made to look silly in front of a hysterical throng of fellow passengers.

Like Chris, I spent many years at boarding school in South Africa; suffered the new boy rituals and felt the cane many many times. These were the realities of life back then and Chris tells many fascinating stories about these early days which were our reality.

What I like so much about this book is how Chris discusses the transformation of South Africa pre and post 1994. The promised Rainbow Nation was a lie from the outset and the manner in which reverse racism is now acceptable and covered up by the fake mainstream media in South Africa is spelt out in so many examples in the book.

The white population is now persecuted in so many ways for the sins of their forefathers with current President Cyril Ramaphosa justifying everything from widespread corruption by his fellow ANC elite to the collapsing health system on "apartheid" or blaming it on Jan van Riebeeck.

Sadly, the Boer/Afrikaner nation is largely just a shadow of their former glory and one wonders how much more persecution they and the white population, in general, have to go through before these

vii

people wake up and take a stand. This fact of race-based persecution in modern South Africa is spelt out in Chris' book.

I loved the book – it gives you a deep and insightful perspective on why South Africa is in such a mess today. From the compromised judicial system to the rabbit hole failures of ineptocracy and kakistocracy to what South Africa could have achieved post-1994 if it had embraced the Singaporean strategy of meritocracy.

Scott Balson

Loving Life

lovinglifetv.com

Preface

After 27 years of ANC rule, South Africa is now literally at the crossroads. The economy is sinking fast and the governing party of the day is determined not to deviate from its current path to destruction and ruin. It is hoped this book will help enlighten people across the world as to the truth of the unfolding realities there.

Understanding the situation is complex and I do my best to paint an unbiased picture of what happened before the end of apartheid and then followed in the ensuing years. Having lived in South Africa (SA) from 1952 until 2019 I believe I am qualified to make a personal judgement on where the country is headed although I am the first to admit that it is often foolhardy to try and predict the future.

I have been a keen student of SA politics over the years and have sadly watched the country's regression since majority rule in 1994. The whole world and I were inspired by what we saw in SA post-1994 when an air of euphoria prevailed. In the ensuing years, however, I learnt from personal experience about the more negative aspects and in particular, gained many insights after reading RW Johnson's 2015 book titled *How Long will South Africa Survive?*

This book comments on some of the questions posed in Johnson's book, with the addition of my thoughts and observations. Ideally, I recommend reading Johnson's publication beforehand.

Many South Africans have read or heard about Alan Paton's classic book *Cry the Beloved Country*. This was written in the earlier days of the apartheid era. For all the wrongs and sadness of those times, it appears the now looming disaster facing SA will cause history to reflect on a country that held so much promise and has since been relegated to third world status by the current corrupt and incompetent government, hence the title of this book, *Mourn the Beloved Country*.

Christopher R Cornish

Chapter 1

Family Move from England to South Africa

I was born in London, England in June 1951, the third-born and only son in our family, following my two older sisters respectively born in 1948 and 1949, a short time after the end of World War II. We were all born at St. Mary's Hospital in North West London, as were our parents before us. An interesting aside is that in 1948 my mother was in the same hospital as Queen Elizabeth who was giving birth to Prince Charles. The Queen gave all the mothers in the maternity ward a garment for their child. Sadly, this was lost in the sands of time.

After we emigrated to SA in 1952 my parents had two more daughters, both born in Johannesburg. My father who served in the Royal Navy for the last 3 years of the great war and my mother who was in the WRNS met when the fighting ended and married in 1947.

Our parents, Peter and Pearl, on their wedding day – 1947

My father studied accountancy and qualified as a chartered accountant in double-quick time. In those days you were not paid while you served articles of clerkship which were a compulsory part of your training. It was a struggle to survive after the devastation of the war, when food rationing was the order of the day, so, when he was offered a position overseas by his employers Deloitte and Co, one of the big four international accounting firms in the world, my parents decided to take the plunge and make the move. The firm had offices in both Johannesburg SA and Sydney Australia apart from its head office in London.

My father opted for the Johannesburg position not knowing too much about the country and that the apartheid years were only then beginning; the National Party had taken power in 1948. SA was a rapidly developing country as was Australia and neither suffered the devastation of bombing raids that England endured. Thus, to make the move meant an immediate improvement in our standard of living. He chose SA because it was a lot closer to home compared to Australia halfway around the world. In those days the cheapest mode of travel was by boat. The commercial aviation industry was still in its infancy and not considered all that safe.

As the saying goes life is all about choices and if he had picked Sydney, our lives would have been vastly different, and I certainly would not be putting pen to paper having spent most of my life without any reason to become embroiled in SA politics.

We departed for our new country aboard the Warwick Castle in June 1952 when I was one year old. We disembarked in Durban from where, years later I learned we travelled to Johannesburg by road.

The Warwick Castle, 1952

Chapter 2

Growing up under apartheid; the early years

Our first home was a rented house in the older but fairly central modest suburb of Parkhurst in Johannesburg.

My earliest recollection of life is when at the age of about three and a half I managed to injure myself quite badly while playing with my mother's new Singer Sewing machine when the needle stabbed my fingers several times. In those days my mother used to make most of our clothes because this was the more affordable option.

When I was four my father bought an undeveloped property in the new suburb of Berario and had plans drawn up to build a new house. I still have the old title deeds to the property. The conveyancing secretary in those days had to be an extremely accurate typist, using a portable typewriter, and bashing hard to get the letters typed onto the four carbon copies beneath the original.

While this house was being built, we went back to England for six months and resided in a cottage overlooking the village green in tiny Woldingham, Surrey. The reason for staying there was because my mother's parents owned a supermarket on the main road on the other side of the village green. There I was enrolled in a nursery school for the first time while my two older sisters attended the local primary school.

My maternal great grandmother who I only ever met once, in Woldingham, 1961

My two older sisters, Tina and Mary with me in Woldingham – 1956

On our return to Johannesburg, we moved into our new home at 194 Delores Avenue, Berario. It consisted of three bedrooms, one bathroom, a lounge, dining room and kitchen and had a single garage. This housed my father's old Citroen which was similar to the vehicles driven by German officers in World War II.

My two younger sisters were born while living there. We all went to Northcliff Primary School up the road which was within walking distance although I often cycled to school. Of course, there were no black school pupils and the only contact we had with black people was seeing a few housemaids, helpers who would attend to the domestic cleaning and washing for those whites who could afford such a luxury and the occasional black gardener, likewise only for the fortunate few. And then they had to carry a pass as they were otherwise not allowed into our white *enclave*. I remember we had a Portuguese boy at our school and he was also regarded as different. Noticeably most of the pupils at Northcliff Primary were English-speaking whereas white Afrikaans-speaking children mostly went to Fairlands Primary School. We used to have an annual game of football (soccer) against them. We would always win as they played rugby only and used to just kick the ball forward which invariably cost them possession and the game.

In those days we had no idea of how the world was going to develop but I remember a teacher, Mr Mason, telling us that one day we would be able to go to work reading the newspaper while the car steered itself. We all thought he was *cuckoo* and yet now this is very close to reality.

When we moved into our Berario house it was one of only a few that had been built and there was long yellow grass-covered veld all around us. The grass was tall enough for us to hide in as children. As the suburb grew and developed, we saw more and more black faces, mostly those who were employed in the construction industry for new houses. Under the pass laws, they had to get back to their homes in the townships with their passes signed by the employer before curfew each day or face arrest and prosecution. The crime rate was extremely low and we never heard of houses being burgled or other serious crimes such as assaults, murders and so forth taking place. We all lived in a bubble. The apartheid regime imposed strict censorship measures and controlled what was read and seen in all media; there was no TV allowed in SA until 1976. In the 1960s our main entertainment was listening to the radio, and some of the programs we enjoyed were *Mark Saxon, no place to hide..., Kid Grayson Rides the Range, Captain Silver, Consider Your Verdict and Squad Cars.* The only criminal incident I can recall during the seven years we lived in Berario was my sister's bicycle being stolen when she left it at the bottom of the driveway: mind you, it could have been stolen by anyone regardless of colour as few people in those days were affluent.

As children, we were often sent to the local shopping centre about a 5-minute walk from the house to buy bread, milk and other necessities. I would notice how a few black men would congregate on an undeveloped plot which we used to take a shortcut. They would mostly gamble while playing a dice game. I do not know whether it was the gambling or the pass laws – I suspect the latter –

but the SA police would frequently raid them and they would scatter in all directions.

One day we were playing in our back garden when about half a dozen black people ran from the shopping area in our direction and jumped over the fence into the garden to avoid detection and of course, we were terrified and ran into the house. This was in about 1960 and probably the first time I realised that all was not well.

While I was at Northcliff Primary I was more interested in cricket and football than my school work. We went on a school bus to play away matches. I remember travelling to Greenside Primary to play a football match. I was the goalkeeper for my sins and the opposition were the kingpins of the Johannesburg Primary School Soccer League and we managed to lose by 8 goals to nil, but what I recall most about the bus trip was when we stuck our heads out the windows and shouted a few swear words at the odd black person we passed, given to us by one of our teammates who knew a few choice Zulu words. This was probably the first time I was influenced to regard black people as *the enemy*. I had so little contact with black people as my mother did her own housework and my father was a keen gardener with the result, they never employed black people.

Childhood adventures included when my two older sisters and I caught a bus to the centre of Johannesburg, a distance of about 12 km, to watch a movie. Walking around the city centre was safe even for primary school children, indicative at the time of the full force of the apartheid regime. When my parents went out in the evening we were left to our own devices and it was not necessary to employ a babysitter despite our young ages. Johannesburg has electric thunderstorms nearly every evening in summer, usually, a quick downpour, after which the weather clears for the rest of the evening. I recall us cowering in fear one night when the lightning flashed and lit the whole sky and thunder reverberated.

On a Saturday morning, we would drive in our new Simca Aronde car to the municipal market in the city centre to buy fresh produce for the week, and there we saw no black shoppers. Our incentive to go along was the reward of a fresh cream doughnut for the return trip. On Saturday evenings we often visited the Veldskoen Drive-In Movie Theatre, cars parked in rows with individual audio speakers clipped to their door windows, all facing a huge screen, and the children often seated on the tarmac in front of the car for a better view. The first movie I can recall watching there was *Jonah and the White Whale.*

Just outside our suburb, there was a wooded area where we often played cops and robbers, cowboys and Indians, made ourselves bows and arrows, and never once had any problem with our safety. I guess that was also indicative of the apartheid era and the fact that in the world as we now know it one has to be more cautious.

In April 1961 we went on a lengthy family holiday overseas. My father was entitled to long leave and the school agreed to us children being absent for a whole term, the second quarter of the year from April to June. The Principal instructed us to keep a daily diary but after a week or so this seemed too much like hard work and the diary was forgotten. We travelled seven-up in our Simca – three in the front and four in the back, my youngest sister only two years of age. Excitedly, we spent a day in the Kruger National Park looking at wildlife. The hot air was laden with dust from the dirt roads at the time. On entering the park we searched for a wild animal and after some time spotted a lone impala. It did not take long to become bored when we later saw thousands of impalas – with not a lion or elephant in sight.

Impala in the Kruger National Park

From there we travelled to a palatial colonial mansion in the heart of hot, humid Lourenço Marques which was later to be renamed Maputo, after those of Portuguese descent (the whites) were given their marching orders, 48 hours to leave or be shot, notwithstanding lifetimes spent developing their country of birth, Mozambique.

The use of the mansion for 3 days was given to us by a Deloitte client before we embarked on the Durban Castle bound for Genoa, Italy via the east coast of Africa and the Suez Canal. What I recall of Lourenço Marques from those days was a beautiful city with predominantly white Portuguese people and pristine palm-lined beaches. Known as LM, it was the trendiest destination for holidaymakers and was the closest city to the sea from

Johannesburg. In 2006 when I visited Maputo again, the change in the city was shocking; dilapidated and dirty with washing hanging out of the windows of the high-rise buildings erected in the colonial era. We were warned against using the city beaches because of all the broken glass littering the beaches and the sea itself. Further along the coastline, I saw the aftermath of the civil war, many blackened burnt-out buildings and walls pockmarked with high-velocity bullet holes.

Back to the Durban Castle, we were in tourist class and our swimming pool was a dropdown canvas "bag" above the cargo hold of the ship, with the proper pool reserved for first-class passengers only. The highlight of the day for all the children was when the crew dished out vanilla ice cream cups, and there were always seconds or even thirds for us. Sailing up the east coast one of the first ports of call was Beira. Ashore we caught a bus from the town centre to the beach on the other side of the bay. The bus was jam-packed and rather conspicuously we were the only white people on it. After alighting, one of my older sisters remarked that the bus *smelled*, probably the result of the influence of her white peers in SA at the time.

We eventually arrived in Genoa after a month aboard. My father refused to disembark until they found our Simca which the captain insisted was not on the ship, against which my father argued he had seen the car descending by crane into the hold. It was finally located at the bottom of the cargo hold – there were steel bars across which the cargo was loaded in layers – and the ship's departure for England was delayed by a whole day as a result. The Simca took us down to Naples where we stayed with my aunt and uncle who were living there at the time. Their son, my cousin, impressed me with a 1,000 Lire note, although I did not know then this was only worth about one pound. From there we motored and ferried to England where we renewed our acquaintance with verdant green Woldingham. It struck me how green England was compared to SA.

11

After visiting family in Cornwall, where I picked wild mushrooms with my grandfather, we eventually returned to SA from Southampton on the Edinburgh Castle. This time, we docked in Cape Town before the long 900-mile drive back to Johannesburg, 7-up in our Simca.

Cape Town, the Mother City

As the ship prepared to sail, accompanied by tugs and a smaller pilot boat, the Union-Castle Line (which also owned the Durban Castle among others similarly named) loud theme music played over the ship's loudspeakers on deck, a catchy tune I still remember although I never learned the title of this music. A highlight of both cruises was my sisters and I winning the fancy dress competitions after my father dressed us up as the lady and the gardener from Lady Chatterley's Lover, a book banned in SA by the apartheid regime for being too risqué although, of course, this was completely lost on us as children but never failed to amuse the spectators. For my two older sisters and me, our last week on this cruise was spent in the ship's hospital where we were treated for chickenpox.

My eldest sister, Tina, and me winning the Fancy Dress Competition on board
Edinburgh Castle – 1961

It was in 1961 that SA became a republic, independent of Britain, and adopted the decimal Rand currency. For the sake of reference, the "Rand" currency of SA will be referred to by its usual abbreviation to "R" below.

In June the following year, 1962, I went on a school camp tour to Rhodesia as it was known then. We visited all the major tourist

13

attractions, including the internationally-renowned Zimbabwe Ruins, which showed that the original King of Zimbabwe (and his ascendants) had established a city state which operated successfully for centuries, which traded with the Arabs and Chinese. When the rich seams of gold petered out, and elephant tusks were no longer as easily available to the Zimbabweans, for fear of their nation being enslaved by the Arab traders, the King made a deliberate choice to leave all the fine granite palaces and other grand buildings, and effectively, the Zimbabweans migrated to ensure their safety.

The Zimbabwe Ruins – with acknowledgment to Time Inc.

And, of course, we also visited the magnificent Victoria Falls in all its splendour. I remember visiting Salisbury and it was pristine, certainly compared to today's Harare (after being renamed) which has become just another dilapidated African city.

The Victoria Falls in Zimbabwe

In May 1963, my father was offered the position of financial director of the famous baby powder company Johnson & Johnson which had a factory in East London on the southern coast of SA. He was reluctant to leave the accountancy profession and shortly thereafter was made a partner at Deloitte South Africa. This meant relocating to Port Elizabeth also on the coast some 1,000 km from Johannesburg.

PE, as it is affectionately known, is also a windy city of which fact my primary school teacher at Northcliff informed me – he was certainly correct. PE was also the major motor manufacturing city boasting huge Ford, General Motors and Volkswagen factories.

So, in June 1963 we departed for the coast after selling our Berario home for £4,750 a small profit over the £4,500 it cost. Inflation was very low in those days and after 7 years the increase in value was minimal. Had my father chosen the J&J East London position again shows how simple choice might have resulted in a rather different

Christopher R Cornish

life.

Chapter 3

Port Elizabeth and the next phase

We as children were very reluctant to make the move to PE, having to change schools midway through the year. Initially, we all felt that we preferred Johannesburg. Our first week in PE was spent at the King Edward Hotel, built during Victorian times with a grand arched entrance through which horse-drawn carriages had entered.

My parents bought a 5-bedroom, 2-bathroom home in Mill Park, one of the best suburbs in the city for the princely sum of R12,600 to house our large family.

SA had in 1961 when it became a republic, abandoned British Sterling and adopted the Rand currency.

I was enrolled at Grey Junior School, a walk of a mere 500 yards from our home. I only spent six months at the school as I could not gain admission to the High School of the same name for the 1964 academic year, not having written the June exams which were an entrance exam to the Grey High School. Despite my father's protests to the school board and the education department, we were advised the school was full. It was a question of who one knew and we were new to the city.

My father was always keen for me to attend a boarding school to get me away from my sisters and it was off to Dale College in King William's Town for me, after applying to various boarding schools. Dale was the first to accept me and so it was we set off on the car trip of some 3 hours to get there.

Those years passed very slowly, with me continually homesick and counting down the days to the school holidays which were never long enough. I had to go through the initiation rituals of new boys for their first year, which included the initiates forming a human *chariot* to carry the big rugby players, with inevitable collapse after a few yards, torn trousers, scratches and abrasions, accompanied by punches and jibes. I had to carry an *old pot's* books to and from school each day, apart from making his (and my) bed each day before breakfast, having to walk to the shop to buy whatever he ordered, and there were times I was part of a line-up of younger boys facing the wall while the bigger boys hit tennis balls at us as hard as they could from a few yards away. Murphy's Law, the headmaster died of a heart attack in December that year, and from the time of the new headmaster's appointment onwards, all initiation and bullying were outlawed with immediate effect. The teachers took a sadistic delight in caning the new boys if there was any noise during homework prep time or after lights out, and it was almost impossible to avoid getting these *cuts.*

Of course, at boarding school, even with the new headmaster it was still the survival of the fittest with the inevitable bullying that took place. We had a Jewish pupil in our dormitory ostracised to such an extent that he left after his first year. I can just imagine what went on in the boarding houses when years later black pupils were first admitted to the school. These days the situation has changed completely with 95% of the pupils now black.

Before 1994 there was a scandalous report in the media and some pupils were expelled from the school after they were caught bunking from the hostel late at night and assaulted some black people *for fun.*

Halfway through my senior year, there was one pupil at the hostel who was considered to be an expert in politics and, of course, he espoused the apartheid policies of the ruling National Party government.

We used to travel to and from Port Elizabeth by train and one day as we pulled out of the station in the small town of Alice, a black in the crowd of people on the platform spat into our open window and unfortunately, the blob of spittle landed on me. This was *the end of the world* and I had to wash several times to remove this *poison* from a black person, such was our conditioning at the time. At this stage, I did not have a particular opinion about SA politics although I was well aware the blacks were not allowed to do numerous things such as using *our* beaches, park benches, post offices and other public amenities.

When I left school at the end of 1968, I found a temporary job at a local bottle store. In line with all liquor outlets, the store had to have separate *Whites Only* and *Non-White* entrances and exits. This was the law. I was about to embark on my tertiary education at the local university and it was around this time I it struck me we were living in a crazy country with ridiculous racial laws.

Chapter 4

University and the political transition period

After leaving school I was supposed to undergo compulsory military training, mainly due to the nationalist government's perceived threat of the *communist onslaught*. As things turned out it was more a question of maintaining the *status quo* in neighbouring countries and thereby SA's borders – thus keeping the *swart gevaar* (black danger) at bay.

I applied to enlist in the Navy having naval connections through my father. To my horror, I was posted to the SA Infantry Corps in Potchefstroom, a predominantly Afrikaans town and nationalist stronghold in the Western Transvaal. I could not see myself marching for a year to achieve nothing but some physical fitness and more particularly so, as I did not see this increasing militarisation and endeavour to maintain border security had anything to do with me. I then applied to join the SA Navy's permanent force as opposed to the citizen force. In the PF the pay was substantially more and what many young men did was buy their way out by paying a lump sum after a year. This counted as having completed one's compulsory military conscription. As it happened perfect eyesight was a prerequisite for acceptance into the Navy. That I did not have and lo and behold, after completing the medical examination, I received a notification in the post that I was medically unfit – because I had a weaker left eye – this certificate was hastily dispatched by me to the Head of the armed forces in Pretoria. A telegram reply was sent to me to say I was exempt from all further military duty.

The armed forces were only for white people and most of the officers were Afrikaans-speaking and by implication staunch nationalists. As I alluded to above, racism has many forms, not only white on black and later black on white but also against religious and different language-speaking groups.

Sometime later I was told of an incident by a friend who happened to be Jewish, while he was doing his military training. This was related as a hilarious anecdote but would not have been so funny for him at the time. To appreciate it, one needs to have an understanding of Afrikaans. What happened at roll call was the sergeant major read out his name in his Afrikaans accent as *Beerman* instead of Burman. Of course, he failed to acknowledge being present. When later the sergeant major queried my friend's *absence,* he provided the correct pronunciation of his name, being Burman. In typical fashion of any sergeant major, his reply was, and I quote *Dan is jy seker 'n fokken Joodse akker piel.* I will leave anyone unfamiliar with Afrikaans to either guess the meaning or google the somewhat unprintable translation.

Rather than waste a year it was decided I should enrol at the local university, although my father was willing to send me to any university I chose. The University of Port Elizabeth had only been going for a few years and was seen as the first model dual-language-medium university with half of the subjects being taught in Afrikaans and the remainder in English. It appeared that most of my legal subjects were in Afrikaans and certainly almost all of my lecturers were Afrikaans-speaking, at the time also somewhat of a blessing in disguise. I left school having passed Afrikaans as a (compulsory) major subject but had very little experience of the spoken word. I quickly learned to become conversant in Afrikaans through its daily use at university, even though the economic subjects for my B. Com law degree had more English lecturers.

In April 1969, my two older sisters got married at the ages of 18 and 19, something unheard of today. Although my father was against the idea, it reduced our family budget substantially and paying for my university education became a breeze. This was more so as universities were heavily subsidised by the government and nowhere near as expensive as today. It was also easier to gain admission at the whites-only university with fewer people competing for places. Incidentally, my two sisters were married in different churches on the same day and had one big combined reception. Happily, they are both still married and have celebrated their golden anniversaries.

During my early years of university, I became far more aware of politics and was influenced the most by my father. He had become well known in the PE business community as a senior partner in Deloitte and Co Port Elizabeth. He was responsible for the General Motors account (which Deloitte handled worldwide), a huge and important one.

Growing up in Johannesburg I do not know whether I was too young (at age 10) or it was the fact that we were shielded from events taking place in SA (by heavy-handed government censorship) but I never heard of the 1961 Sharpeville massacre; 69 black people including eight women and ten children were shot and killed by the police, and 180 people injured, in the name of quelling an uprising. In 1976 I experienced the first real political violence when on the 16th of June that year there was more shooting by the police of schoolchildren who staged demonstrations against the introduction of Afrikaans into their school curriculum. According to the official figure, 176 people, mainly students, were killed as the rioting spread across the nation, but unofficial estimates are as high as 700 dead. Deloitte and Co were instructed by the Attorney General to investigate certain high-profile fraud cases, and I recall two cases in particular, the State vs Parity Insurance and the State vs Marks, in which my father was responsible for leading forensic evidence in court. As will appear later from reading this book, the current government no longer displays the slightest interest in using auditors in such cases. June the 16th was, however, commemorated as an annual public holiday, Youth Day, when the ANC came to power, a decision that met with everyone's approval.

In the early-1970s I played a lot of competitive interclub golf and one of the clubs visited was a club named Wedgwood, with a large predominantly Jewish membership. By the late 1970s, many of these Jewish doctors, lawyers, architects and other professionals had left or were leaving SA for fear of the future; most of them immigrated to Australia. Many observers commented that when Jewish people start packing up and leaving, it's time to take notice.

My father always maintained that SA needed to create a middle-class black society to stabilise the country. To achieve this required removal of ridiculous apartheid laws, including the blacks not being allowed to own property, reform of the education system and integration of black people into the monetary system. His other firm belief was that economics would always prevail and determine the future path of the country. This is discussed in detail later. He became increasingly concerned by the political situation, so much so that he set up an overseas trust fund and steadily increased its value whenever he could, although at the end of the day it did not amount to a fortune. Sadly, he was to pass away in 1984 from pancreatic cancer three months short of his 60th birthday. He and I had many political discussions in the late 1970s and early 1980s and it was a pity he never lived to see the changes that took place leading to 1994. However, he would certainly not have been enamoured by the post-apartheid developments with the ANC government slowly but surely grinding the country into the dirt.

In 1970 I voted in my first election when we had the choice between the governing National Party and the United Party, the main opposition party led by Sir de Villiers Graaff who was knighted by the Queen, and the Progressive Party led by the anti-apartheid activist Helen Suzman. Most Afrikaners voted for the government while most English speakers voted for the United Party, a slightly more left-wing party. The Progressive Party was a very minor player at that stage and was seen as being *too liberal*. I opted for the United Party at the time but soon changed course to the left.

I had a good Afrikaans friend who at that stage was a government supporter and worked for a government department before he started his studies in PE and majored in industrial psychology. I would often discuss with him the fact that the country could not indefinitely continue on its current course and that left-wing reforms

23

were necessary. He eventually changed his thinking completely to agree with me. He was made a senior lecturer at the University of Fort Hare in that same small town of Alice I mentioned previously. The government had built a university there, out of the way and exclusively for blacks. My friend subsequently became a professor a few years later back at the University of Port Elizabeth. The government built universities outside the major cities in the country exclusively for people of colour in furtherance of its separate development policies. In my hometown of PE, they built another university in the township areas named Vista University.

The next election was in 1974 and the Progressive Party had grown substantially at the expense of the United Party which was going nowhere and eventually disappeared. The Progressive Party got my vote. A senior law colleague and fellow attorney, Manny Goldberg was the constituent United Party member, quite a character with a cigar permanently dangled from his lips, who believed we would vote for him not knowing there was little chance of that. Before the election, the parties put numerous posters on lamp and telephone poles depicting the candidates and seeking votes for them. In PE, there is a main road called Target Kloof and late one night shortly before the election another friend and I pulled down all the National Party posters, throwing these onto the back seat of our car. At the top of the road, we stopped to put all the posters in the boot. This proved to be a lifesaver as shortly thereafter two Afrikaans-speaking policemen stopped their police van next to us and enquired if everything was *alright*. After looking inside our car they never thought to inspect the boot. Had they done so we faced arrest and probable jail time.

After graduating with my B. Com law degree in 1971, I entered into articles of clerkship in 1972 and simultaneously did a B. Proc degree through the University of South Africa, a correspondence-only university. After qualifying as an attorney in 1974 and a property conveyancer and a notary public the following year, I worked as a professional assistant in legal practice for a few years until 1977, when I went cruising again with a friend; we caught the second-last voyage of the Transvaal Castle from PE, arriving in Southampton 12 days later. I had also been to England two years earlier in 1975 but only for a short three-week holiday. In 1977 it was for six months and a fact-finding mission on how to become a legal practitioner in the United Kingdom.

Before leaving, I worked for a law firm Ward-Able and Gibson, the senior partner a long-standing member of the local city council who spent one day a week on council meetings which, in those days was for no remuneration being considered an honour to serve the community, such a contrast to today. Not only has the number of councillors trebled, but they are today paid astronomical salaries.

At that time SA had very few qualified black attorneys. I had befriended a mixed-race attorney of my age through discussing the situation in the country during our waiting times at court, and we agreed that politically things would have to change. Another colleague used to joke that the *Revolution* was coming. We all knew change was inevitable. It was only a question of when and how. After travelling around the UK and Europe in an old VW Kombi, I decided my legal career lay in SA and returned home. What also influenced my decision at the time was the fact that a lady I fancied had found a new boyfriend overseas and she ended up staying in London for nearly 4 years before having to return home as she was not a British citizen. At the beginning of 1978, the SA economy was not in great shape and in particular the property market – the specialisation legal field I had chosen – was not doing well. No jobs were going at the time and a golfing friend of mine who was a public prosecutor and I decided to open a law practice as partners, with the blessing of my father who agreed to organise the required finance for us.

One of my first conveyancing jobs was to attend to the transfer of an upmarket suburban property which bordered on our local golf course. The owner was a fellow golf member, a Welsh doctor who emigrated to SA to join a local practice in 1975 and subsequently decided to return to Wales in 1978. He had purchased the property for R54,000 but sold it three years later for R47,000, such was the state of the economy. The political situation was deteriorating and must have played a part in his decision. My father in 1978 decided that the outlook had improved and subsequently sold the Mill Park house for R39,000 and bought an English-style cottage house on an acre of land with a tennis court and swimming pool for R65,000 in the best part of town. In 1979 and 1980 the property market had a huge upswing due to the economy improving thanks largely to ongoing increases in the gold price. I remember at the time the Governor of the Reserve Bank publicly urging people to *go out and spend* to kickstart the economy. Prices of everything rose across the board and inflation kicked in.

A few months after returning from overseas I met my future wife, Denise who had been born and lived in PE all her life. We have five daughters including a set of twins. I never intended to have a large family but I *inherited* my eldest daughter, Leanne from my wife's first marriage and after our firstborn daughter, Catherine, Denise gave birth to twins, Lara and Michelle. Unbelievably, they respectively weighed 9 lbs 4 oz and 8lbs 3 oz, a total birth weight of 17 lbs 7 oz, apparently a record at the Sandford Maternity Home which still stands today (although the Home does not). The doctor told us Denise would not fall pregnant again without fertility drugs. But lo and behold, another baby arrived, five daughters in total. I hurriedly then got myself *sorted out* – in the form of a vasectomy.

Our marriage took place four months after Denise and I first met. Our wedding reception was held in the garden of my parents' new home. Happily, everything has worked out well between us. After my father's sudden passing in 1984, we moved into my parents' family home as my mother opted to stay with my second-eldest sister, Mary. Life was good but things were changing rapidly as violence increased and bombs started going off; none of us knew whether they were planted by the far right or the far left of the political spectrum.

Of course, the world was changing and the anti-racism movement in the western world had gained momentum. America had its own *apartheid* until changes began in the 1960s when persons like Rosa Parks and Martin Luther King had an impact on changing the *status quo*. Economic sanctions were introduced and as Johnson pointed out these were to be a deciding factor in effecting a regime change rather than the ANC trying to play at war games. The National Party was firmly in control of the country and could have maintained the status quo for a long time to come; but things would have become very messy if a negotiated settlement was not reached.

In 1989 FW de Klerk had taken over from PW Botha as President after Botha failed to deliver on his promise of change in his infamous Rubicon speech. In 1992, De Klerk held a referendum of the solely white electorate on ending apartheid. I voted *Yes*. As did nearly 70% of the country's whites.

SA is a sports-mad country and after the 1981 *flour bomb* rugby tour of New Zealand, countries across the world refused to have any further sporting contact with SA. A few years earlier England cancelled a cricket tour to SA (which had long before been kicked out of the Olympic games). The cricket was cancelled because the apartheid government refused to accept the selection of a former SA cricketer, Basil d'Oliviera, to play for the England team, based purely on the colour of his skin; notwithstanding that he had qualified to play for his adopted country as a talented batsman. This angered a large section of the English-speaking community in the country and it seemed that as long as the Afrikaner section still had international rugby, everything was considered well. He later proved his worth on the international stage, despite the nationalist government regarding his selection as *window-dressing*.

The first real change occurred when Nelson Mandela was released from prison unconditionally in 1990 and all South Africans had their first glimpse of what he looked like in person, hardly the fearsome terrorist who had been locked away for 27 years. Significantly, prisoners who got life imprisonment for heinous crimes such as murder and rape were eligible for parole after 20 years. With the release of Mandela, the negotiation of the new Constitution got

27

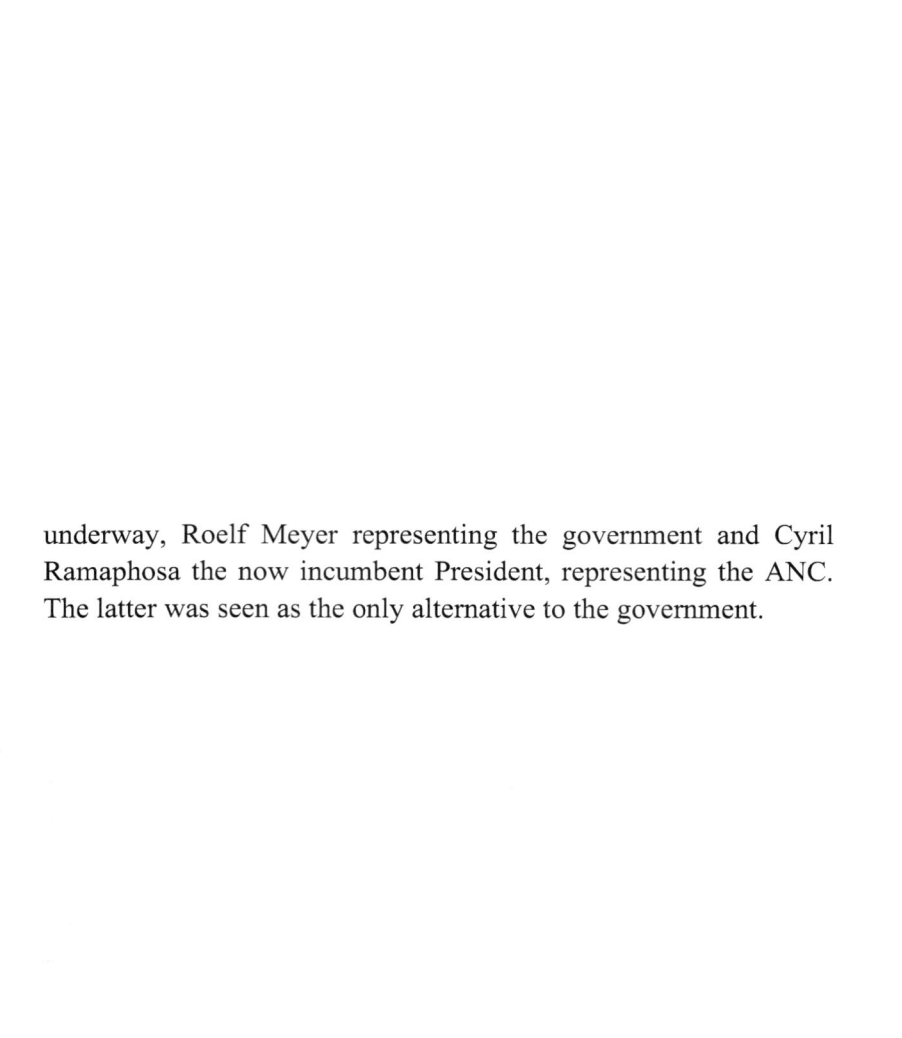

underway, Roelf Meyer representing the government and Cyril Ramaphosa the now incumbent President, representing the ANC. The latter was seen as the only alternative to the government.

Chapter 5

Preparing for the first majority election onwards

The drafting of the Constitution involved a lot of time and effort and obviously, there had to be concessions made on both sides. But as would be seen in years to follow it is impossible to safeguard everyone's rights and interests. The new Constitution was eventually passed into law in 1997, quite long after the 1994 national and local elections; the ANC was the majority party ruling at the time under a government of national unity with De Klerk as the Vice President and Mandela as the President.

The election forecasts proved correct, the ANC romped home with more than a two-thirds majority. The National Party eventually disappeared along with the United Party and the left-wing party I had always supported became the official opposition party from the 1999 election onwards, under the guise of the Democratic Alliance (DA).

In the early days of ANC rule the party did not need to change the Constitution and in subsequent elections lost its two-thirds majority thus putting paid to any such notions.

Nelson Mandela retired as he had promised after one term in office. He was in any event already 77 and his life imprisonment was taking its toll on him. Thabo Mbeki was his designated successor and took over after the second election. During Mandela's term, there was the euphoria of the Springboks winning the Rugby World Cup in 1995, people of all colours united and dancing in the streets. One has to praise President Mandela for playing a huge role in uniting the country at the time. Unfortunately, the euphoria of winning a major trophy does not last very long and once rid of the celebratory hangover, the realities of life set in all too soon.

The dream of a rainbow nation has sadly long since evaporated. Mandela introduced affirmative action black empowerment policies, arguably the number one reason for SA's economic mess today plus the entrenchment of *reverse racism* – despite the original ANC Freedom Charter espousing a non-racial society – and the now-endemic cronyism. Based purely on who they know, people who are inadequately educated, incapable and inexperienced are put into top management positions, with failure the only prospect.

Perhaps the London Times Quote of the Week best sums up the situation:

Interesting point of view Affirmative Action: "South Africa is the only country in the world where affirmative action is in the favour of the majority who has complete political control. The fact that the political majority requires affirmative action to protect them against a 9% minority group is testament to a complete failure on their part to build their own wealth-making structures, such that their only solution is to take it from others."

And finally, a word to define South Africa's current political situation. Ineptocracy: - a system of government where the least capable to lead are elected by the least capable of producing, and where the members of society least likely to sustain themselves or succeed, are rewarded with goods and services paid for by the confiscated wealth of a diminishing number of producers.

Mbeki's *reign* was well documented by Johnson and apart from continuing socialist policies towards ruination, he will be remembered for his blunders on the HIV AIDS crisis, his pro-stance on Zimbabwe and his insistence that Mugabe was a *hero* (and we all know what happened to Zimbabwe under Mugabe). There were also Mbeki's stubborn continued support for his Health Minister, nicknamed *Dr Beetroot* for advocating that AIDS sufferers would be cured by eating beetroots, and for his national police chief and Interpol boss at the time, Jackie Selebi who was eventually imprisoned. To crown it all he wanted to change the Constitution so he could stay in power for a third presidential term.

With the notable exception of Mandela, why African leaders think they have a divine right to stay in power for life is beyond comprehension when supposedly living in a modern democracy conforming to Western norms. The Zulu faction in the ANC was having none of this and immediately hatched plans to oust Mbeki by having him *recalled*. Mbeki had fired his Zulu Vice President Jacob Zuma when a charge of rape was laid against him. Some said Mbeki had trumped up these charges to justify getting rid of Zuma. In any event, Zuma was acquitted at his trial and the truth concerning the whole matter will probably only be known by very few including certainly the woman who laid the charge. Suffice it to say that after this trial, the rape complainant had to flee SA for her life following many death threats.

Zuma's infamous evidence at his rape trial was that he did not use a condom because a simple shower after sex was enough to wash away any chance of an AIDS infection.

In the ANC, there is an elective conference held every five years, to elect a national executive committee (NEC). In practice, the president of the ANC automatically becomes the President of the country. After Mbeki's *resignation,* the next-in-line within the NEC was Kgalema Motlanthe who replaced Mbeki to serve as the country's third SA President from September 2008 until May 2009. Widely considered a caretaker president on behalf of Zuma, Mothlante only lasted in office for a short stay until Jacob Zuma won the presidency of the ANC, then became President of South Africa.

Thus in 2009, SA had the misfortune to have Zuma as its first Zulu president. For the next 9 years, he wrecked the SA economy and caused *his people* so much poverty and misery it defies logic or belief. Mandela was insistent a Zulu be made the next President (following Mbeki, also of the Xhosa tribe as was Mandela) and Zuma was his man, despite being uneducated yet still rewarded for a few years spent on Robben Island. The ANC again easily won the elections in 2013, despite the economic and shocking governance

31

disaster of Zuma's first five years in office.

From Prisoner to President to Prisoner – Jacob Zuma

Zuma did exactly what he pleased and plundered the state's coffers aided by the Gupta family masterminding this. According to the SA Council of Churches and various academics, R40 billion (equivalent to US$3 billion) was unlawfully siphoned to Dubai by the Gupta family and associated companies between 2012 and 2017. One cannot help but wonder which banks were involved, taking into account central bank rules on moving funds abroad. Zuma's son, Duduzani seems happy to flaunt *his* wealth in Dubai, fashion models on his arm, flashy cars and Moët & Chandon champagne.

Slowly, the facts began to emerge in the press and in Parliament. He brazenly fired good people and hired sycophants to suit his needs. Jacques Paauw published his book titled *The President's Keepers: Those Keeping Zuma in Power and out of Prison* (2017) in which explicit facts were given setting out Zuma's shenanigans. How he has stayed out of jail for so long and still dodges the legal system even today is mind-blowing. For years he claimed immunity as President of the country and even got the state to pay for his legal expenses for some considerable time. Things finally came to a head when Vice President Cyril Ramaphosa persuaded Zuma to step down one year before his presidency was to end or face recall and lose his guaranteed lifetime pension, which is the same as his full presidential salary. Ramaphosa, with the backing of high-profile billionaire white businessmen, had a few years earlier survived an ANC election vote for the leadership of the party by narrowly defeating one of Zuma's ex-wives Nkosi Dlamini Zuma. The state continues to support Zuma's four other wives and some 21 children in his enclave Nkandla. After Ramaphosa took over, people were optimistic SA would change course and correct its problems. The country then prepared for its next general election in May 2019 and despite the ANC ruining the economy and making life far worse for its poor masses, numerous people saw the new President as a Saviour. A close member of my family even considered voting for the ANC in this election, my last before departing SA permanently. Reputable journalist Peter Bruce, the former Editor of the well-respected Financial Times and the Business Day newspaper, ostensibly left-wing publications, strongly backed the ANC in the run-up to the election. Disgusted by what I read, I had a few years earlier mentioned to a retired bank manager friend of mine that as long as the ANC ran the country it is doomed to failure.

The 2019 election resulted in the ANC retaining power albeit with a reduced majority but still holding a staggering 57% of the vote. The official opposition DA lost votes. This was a surprise to most but not to me, as many enlightened people of all races had already left the country for greener pastures. Adverse media publicity (read state propaganda) against the DA, supposedly in turmoil, was widespread. Another major factor was that at last count there were more than 1,000,000 white people in squatter camps around the country who with no fixed address were not registered and therefore unable to vote. These squatters, mainly a product of the official policy of there being no jobs for whites, are forced to accept their lot in life. Also, the old right-wing white voters deserted the DA in favour of the Freedom Front Party, going back to their Afrikaner roots. This was senseless given the fact that the party does not play any meaningful role in parliament. The most worrying aspect of the election result is the rise of the radical left-wing party known as the Economic Freedom Fighters (EFF) led by Julius Malema. In the previous election, he garnered 6% of the vote, which doubled to almost 12% in 2019.

So, onwards it is into a bleak and uncertain future, nearly three years of the Cyril Ramaphosa presidency having seen nothing concrete done to fix things despite his numerous flowery but meaningless speeches. Things have continued to go from bad to worse. It appears Zuma is perhaps right about feeling *singled out*, the justice system yet again used to remove political opponents, while the whole of the ANC has been guilty of theft, looting state coffers and corruption – it is rotten to the core.

In 2019 my wife and I left SA for England, where four of our five daughters have already lived for many years. The eldest, Leanne, was the first to leave in 1998, a Rhodes University graduate and teacher at Simonstown High School for a year before that; she always wanted to travel, and after working and marrying in England there was no way she would contemplate returning to SA. Michelle graduated as the top student in the human sciences faculty and became a social worker in SA for a year under an incompetent affirmative-action boss who delighted in sending her into dangerous parts of the community, which resulted in her decision to join Leanne in England. Her twin sister Lara followed after her employment and transfer by international shipping company Maersk, which originally employed her as a B.Com graduate. Our youngest daughter, Amy left for London after moving back and forth while completing her Master's degree in Architecture; despite being a top achiever academically, she was quite unable to find employment in SA (except in Johannesburg, where she knew no one and life is perceived as life-threateningly dangerous). In London, she was employed by the world-famous architect, Sir Nicholas Grimshaw, and today works in a firm of more than 100 professional architects. The comparison between the two countries is akin to apples and pears.

Chapter 6

The State of the Nation Address

My *state of the nation* differs drastically from the picture painted by the President every year at the opening of parliament. This so-called SONA has become a fashion statement where the elites try to outspend and outdo each other, boasting outlandish outfits on the Academy Awards-style red carpet. The actual address comprises mainly taking credit for any achievements whether actual or imagined, rather than concentrating on reality and what needs to be done. The government is consistently great on talk, poor on action. For many years now the President's message has been meaningless and not even close to addressing the real state of the nation.

When Zuma took charge, unemployment was rising at a rapid rate, and he promised the country an increase of 5 million jobs over the ensuing five years. Not only did he not deliver on his promise but he cost the country 2 million jobs thus having a score of minus 7 million. Only what might be expected from an uneducated ignoramus masquerading as President. The first three years under Ramaphosa resulted in flowery speeches from the new incumbent with zero progress. Under his *stewardship,* the country is now gripped by a deep recession. The *economic cliff* that Johnson set out is upon SA and the day of reckoning is approaching faster than many people envisaged. Another 4 years of ANC rule on its current trajectory can only prove catastrophic.

The number one responsibility of any government is the safety and wellbeing of its people, a principle also constitutionally entrenched in SA. On this front, the ANC has failed dismally. Law and order have all but broken down. The masses in the townships fear for their lives every day. SA has the highest murder rate in the world if countries involved in drugs and civil wars are excluded. From 2015, when the SA murder rate per 100,000 population was 35.9, by 2020 this had dropped to 33.97 per 100,000. One has a greater risk of death from murder in SA than a soldier on active duty in Afghanistan. The figures show there are now more than twenty-two thousand murders a year. On average, in 2019, 58 people were murdered every day. If other serious crimes such as rape, robbery, hijacking and assaults are included, the violent crime figures are astronomical. Even in the middle and upper-class suburbs crime is out of control. For years now people have been protecting themselves by living in gated communities, behind electric gates and fences, using sophisticated monitoring systems and armed response security companies, employing whatever means possible to try and protect themselves. The security industry is worth billions of Rands annually and forms a significant part of GDP although it should not be a contributor in the first place, let alone making the people poorer by having to pay these unwanted expenses. It has even got to the stage where security companies are employed to protect police stations. Unbelievable, I know, but true. The SA Police Service (SAPS) employs numerous (i.e. a majority of) obese people, including many women in line with its gender equality policy. Policewomen are not suited to the front line of crime on this scale. The result is you can hardly count on the SAPS to save your life or protect your property in a crisis. Apart from this, the general apathetic attitude of most police members is that they have a job, get paid, but need not lift a finger to do anything. In an emergency, the security companies always arrive first on the scene. The police are hampered by a lack of resources; from mismanagement and corruption, to many vehicles without fuel or in disrepair due to lack of maintenance. The same applies to military personnel. Corruption and theft play a major part in the police themselves not rendering the services for which they are paid. Johnson documented that there are so many generals, colonels and high-ranking officials – many additional posts created post-apartheid – who receive enormous salaries and fancy vehicles, yet only heaven knows what they all do.

In the winter of 1998, the SA Army was sent by Nelson Mandela and came off second best in a skirmish with the tiny neighbouring state of Lesotho. Four years after the new SA came into being, the army had rapidly deteriorated to this extent.

In short, one cannot rely on the state in a time of crisis and it has failed dismally in looking after its citizens' safety and security.

Secondly, as far as education is concerned the ANC has again let the nation down. Johnson detailed the huge failings in the system and it is a disgrace the Minister of Education is still in her job after all this time. Mind you, the same can be said for the rest of the cabinet ministers controlling the other portfolios of government. It is not only a matter of government budget inadequacy. It is total mismanagement, lack of teaching and, yes, even the burning down of hundreds of schools by protesters. Most of these destroyed schools have never been replaced. Books and stationery do not reach schools in time for the start of the school year if at all. There is so much teacher absenteeism that pupils are not receiving a proper, if any, education. Pupils are pushed through to the next grade regardless. This mostly applies to the state schools which cater to the masses; there are still many thousands of young children who do not attend school at all, their focus simply on trying to stay alive which includes begging on the streets.

Laughable (if it was not so sad) is that every year the media makes such a big issue about the fact that a particular province has increased its *examination* pass rate from (a dismal) 55% to 57%, yet the school leaving certificate is not worth the paper it is written on. It certainly does not equip any pupil to continue to tertiary education. There are exceptions to the rule, however; SA still has numerous top schools both in the private sector and its so-called Model-C (formerly white) schools. The fees for these schools cost a fortune and only the middle to upper-classes can afford these. The top private schools such as Michaelhouse now cost at least a quarter of a million Rand a year after tax, per child. Only the big earners in the private sector and the top public sector employees who are grossly overpaid for the little to nothing they do, enjoy this privilege. The Model-C schools cost in the region of R50,000 per child annually and this is a huge burden on the middle class trying to educate their children. When it comes to tertiary education the situation is not much better. As the white professors and senior lecturers retire, they are almost entirely replaced by blacks due to affirmative action policies, irrespective of qualification or ability. Standards have dropped to such an extent that the only university degree still recognised worldwide is that of the University of Cape Town (UCT). At the last count, UCT still ranked 278 in the world. The education system simply does not equip the majority to be an asset in the workplace. I had a black client who managed to educate his son at one of the top Model-C schools in PE and after graduating with a B Com degree at the local university, he landed a job courtesy of the affirmative action policy at one of the major Banks. As it turned out, he lasted one year, unable to cope. He did not enjoy the protection he would have had in the public sector.

Thirdly, when it comes to the health sector it is probably in a greater shambles if that is possible. Again, there is a big distinction between the private and the public sectors. In the public sector despite a healthy budget – excuse the pun – the state of hospitals is an absolute disgrace. Most of them are akin to pigsties, inside and out. The waiting time in emergencies is often too long for many who die before they can get proper if any treatment. This is exacerbated by the number of violent crimes including shootings and stabbings. In 2019, one of the local PE hospitals could not treat heart patients because a new machine was 3 months away from delivery. The supply of medicines often runs out. Patients have to queue for long hours to receive medication and are frequently told to return the next day.

I know of people who have taken their own blankets to the hospital and many who have ordered takeaway food, describing what was dished up by the hospital as inedible. And dare I say it but the vast majority of staff are blacks due to that affirmative action policy, who appear to have a challenge, both culturally and personally, given their background and home situation, to maintain the required hospital standards of care and cleanliness. I have been told of patients not being attended to for many hours on end, their bedclothes full of blood or pus. I recently saw a video on YouTube showing monkeys running around a public hospital ward at Addington Hospital in Durban. Talk about vermin...

My wife is a *myasthenia gravis* sufferer. This illness affects breathing and the ability to eat. It is now thankfully in remission. However, she was referred by a private sector neurologist to the public sector to obtain the most expensive medication from the state. There are pockets of excellence and I must say the consultation she had with the specialist neurologist at the public provincial hospital was first-class. This is the exception rather than the rule; most people opt for private hospital care if they can afford this. The public sector pays very well and many doctors seem happy to have a nine-to-five job without the hassles of employing staff and other overheads of private practice. My physician who recently retired at 68, told me about five years ago that he and two other physicians who were older than him wanted to retire but could not do so until the private hospital found suitable replacements. There were no replacements at the time.

The main reason for this was the affirmative action (black empowerment or BEE) policy that excluded top white pupils from gaining entrance to medical schools. The result was and is the same today, that many bright people have left the country and the few who managed to become doctors also sought greener pastures abroad. When I used to transport my wife to the hospital, she faced a long queue but the saving of R3,000 a month on medication made it worthwhile. There was always rubbish strewn over the hospital lawns where people congregate and lounge in the sun. The bins were overflowing, paint peeling off the walls, toilets broken and filthy, sewage leaking and so on without end. Like all things SA, neither maintenance nor upgrades have been done in years or should I say since 1994 when the ANC assumed power. Mismanagement does not adequately describe the situation. About four years ago a private organisation painted a portion of the exterior of this hospital but gave up after running out of funds and willpower. Reverting to the private health sector the same thing applies as in the education system. You will get proper care so long as you can pay for it. The masses are excluded and the private hospitals are mercenary. If you do not have a substantial deposit, without full medical cover you are turned away no matter your medical emergency. And it has to be a guaranteed payment by card or in cash. The private sector health care comes at a huge cost. There are a few medical aid insurance companies still operating; at last count full medical for a couple amounted to the astronomical sum of R12,000 per month, a rise from R7,000 just a few years previously and from about R3,500 a decade ago.

Rising medical costs will be unaffordable for everyone but the wealthiest soon if it hasn't already reached that stage and one can already see the medical aid schemes battling to stay afloat. The ANC, regardless of the near-collapse of the public sector health system, is hell-bent on pushing through its national health scheme. This will be compulsory even if unaffordable for most workers, and employer subsidies will force more job losses, not to mention the parlous state of government financial *management*. The general perception is that this health scheme fund will simply create another pot of money to be plundered by those in power. A draft document provides for the incorporation of all private care into the public health system, so that everyone will be in the same queue for primary care, and only then in line for referral to a specialist. I cannot see the top end of society taking too kindly to this. I understand that the current private hospitals will be nationalised into the public sector and one wonders how the whole scenario will play out in due course. I guess that when the elite in government realise that their own health is compromised, they will probably – like everything else – kick the can down the road and put it on hold. Procrastination, lack of action and lack of maintenance

41

unfortunately rules (in most of Africa).

Fourthly, as I alluded to earlier in this chapter the economic situation looks very bleak. The government is neither able to balance its books nor to prop up the economy. In short, the government is bankrupt – all due to its crazy economic policies. The private sector is not faring much better with the mass emigration of skilled people, lack of opportunities, too much red tape, lack of a proper power supply, the list goes on, all taking a toll. The country has ended up in a situation from which it will be impossible to extricate itself without radical reforms. Taxes are too high. Numerous businesses are simply shutting their doors. A friend who had a family business supplying electrical products for over 50 years had to close the business in 2020 because the only way to get any government order in the pipeline, is by first giving away 51% or more of the business to a black shareholder to *qualify*. Previously, he had acquired a BEE compliance certificate for black employee quotas that incurred a levy payment of R4,000 per month to the government. He was promised certain government business in return but ultimately walked away, having received zero.

Another example of BEE gone wrong was a few years ago when I visited a client in an industrial area and the premises next door had been vacated as the company had closed after only one year; this *entrepreneur* received a SETA grant of R1 million, and the first thing he did was to buy a new Mercedes Benz while he blew the rest of the money on high living and defaulted in his rental payments.

One of my best friends has retired after working as a toolmaker for a company visited by a labour inspector while he was still employed there. The boss was told that the next toolmaker to be employed had to be black. I am reliably informed that this class of worker is all but *extinct* in the country.

Another person I know who operates a finance business told a labour inspector where to get off and that if he ever came back, he would *shoot him*. Two years later no one has returned and he still has not complied with the quota system; although he considers himself one of the lucky ones, the reality is that he faces a fine or imprisonment and even closure of his business.

Manufacturing output has halved under the ANC and this I have seen with my own eyes, driving down the main road in the industrial sector of PE known as Deal Party, where there are numerous empty buildings and for sale or to let signs everywhere. A year ago, my banker told me people were stretched to the limit financially and most clients only visited the bank to extend their credit facilities.

Enough on the economic situation for now but to repeat the obvious: it is in a mess.

It would not go amiss at this stage to discuss the state of the infrastructure in the country. Not only has the ANC never invested in new infrastructure over the years but it has failed to maintain what it inherited from the old regime. The most glaring example is Eskom, the electricity provider for the country. This is a story all on its own. The only time the country spent big money was before hosting the World Cup in 2010. Billions were wasted on building stadiums which are now white elephants. The ring road around Johannesburg was improved at a huge cost and money was supposed to be recovered via the so-called e-Tolls. These would have cost the average working person a fortune to use daily. Most people have stopped paying altogether although only 20% of people ever paid. This is typical of the lack of management on the government's part so much so that I believe there are plans to scrap the tolls altogether. In my hometown of PE millions were spent on a so-called bus rapid transportation system for the World Cup. For over a year this created a total mess and at the end of the day the job was never completed; more than 10 years later there are still investigations and ongoing court cases regarding missing funds. A true debacle led by the ANC municipal council. After the DA took over the reins in 2016 and attempted to rectify the situation, things came to a halt yet again when the coalition was booted out due to the opposition again gaining the upper hand by bribing councillors with remunerative positions if they voted with them, tantamount to them doubling their salaries. The ANC has not across the country invested in any new dams or taken any other steps such as desalination plants to maintain an adequate water supply. As a result, PE had water restrictions for more years than I could remember. It certainly is not worth being an avid gardener. When one does get decent rains to fill the dams it only takes a short while to empty them given not only the increase in the population but the fact that the infrastructure is crumbling and not maintained at all.

A friend of mine was in charge of the water affairs at the PE council and at the time the municipality employed over 35 qualified engineers. When he was overlooked for the top job due to affirmative action he resigned and went into private practice and the black appointee had no idea how to run the department yet was paid the big bucks. The other reason he left was after he was shot in the leg by an employee while chairing a disciplinary hearing, and was lucky to escape with his life. A few years later he advised me the municipality then only employed one qualified engineer.

The big thing is, he explained, that it will now take 30 years' annual maintenance work to restore the system to where it was in 1994. The city loses about 30% of its capacity annually, water pouring out of broken pipes which might or might not be repaired many weeks later. The country was recently fortunate to receive good rains to replenish supplies, except for PE where dam levels remain at a dangerously low 10% and falling.

Kouga Dam
Levels 2018 at 7%

The Kouga Dam, PE's biggest, is now at 4% and steadily falling. Day Zero approaches. Recent rains and flooding (July 2021) have come at the 11th hour but will only provide temporary respite.

The roads are in a poor state with potholes in most towns and cities. The exception to this is the Western Cape which is the only province run by the DA and which generally has good governance unlike the rest of the country. No wonder people have flocked to live in Cape Town. The biggest problem with this influx is Cape Town's cost of housing has now gone through the roof and the traffic is worse than in Johannesburg, SA's biggest city.

Apart from the state of the roads one of the biggest hurdles SA faces is dodging all the other road users. The ubiquitous black taxis do not stop at red lights unless they have no other option, which includes mounting pavements and driving in the wrong lanes to get past other traffic – they also disregard stop (and other) traffic signs. The road accident rate is horrific, if not the highest in the world. Even other road users are now following the example of taxi drivers. When the traffic light turns amber it is time to put your foot on the gas and cater for at least another three vehicles following you through.

Of course, there are no traffic cops to be seen anywhere and if there were they would be too scared to do anything about it. They are about as *extinct* as the black rhino! They only exist to trap other

45

motorists driving a few kilometres over the speed limit, an exercise in futility as most people do not bother to pay their fines. Another friend of mine is an exception to the rule. In his fast car, he regularly picks up speeding fines and recently went with his cheque book in hand to settle what fines he had amassed. He was subsequently stopped at a roadblock and told he owed a substantial amount, which he naturally disputed, only to be informed he should go to the council to ascertain the correct position. At the offices, they could not resolve the issue, advising him that their records were three years behind. No wonder the council is virtually bankrupt. While on the question of traffic police, many years ago the former government purchased 100 top range 1100cc motorcycles for the traffic cops and these could be seen all over PE. No motorist thought of taking a chance, the traffic police were so visible. Of course, they have long since *disappeared* and you will now see only an occasional traffic police car, usually parked outside a Kentucky Fried Chicken outlet. One of my children's godmothers retired to a family home at Coffee Bay on the Transkei coast and we used to take an annual trip to visit her, some 6 hours' drive away.

Coffee Bay in all its splendour.

The stretch of road through the filthy dilapidated towns en route must be about the most dangerous in the world. There are numerous head-on collisions and nothing ever gets done about enforcing road safety.

On our last trip made to see her, we counted seven instances of other vehicles crossing the solid barrier line to overtake our car. What adds to the road carnage is that a large percentage of drivers do not have a valid driving licence. For a small *fee* one can easily obtain a forged licence. No less than the Speaker at Parliament acquired her licence illegally; although undisputed, nothing was ever done about this. In Butterworth, which has reverted to a typical African town, streets cluttered with informal (unlicensed, of course) traders and black taxis driving recklessly, a white motorist's car was hit by a taxi from behind; the drivers went to the nearby police station, where the policemen advised that the motorist opt to pay the R2,000 in damages demanded by the taxi driver. The taxi driver caused the collision but despite this, the motorist went to the ATM and paid the taxi driver rather than risk being shot by the driver, as the policeman had informed him would otherwise be the case. The law of the jungle rules in Africa.

In all major cities, the once-proud centres have become dirty crumbling slums where drug lords roam free. Big business has built new suburban centres outside the original central areas, the only exception being Cape Town, where, being run by the DA, part of their budget is spent correctly. As for the towns in the rest of the country, they are mostly dilapidated, dirty and typical of any African country, filled with informal street traders who mostly live in the huge *townships* on the outskirts of the towns.

The government has, by and large, reneged on its promises to build new houses for the poor and many millions still live in squatter camps and remain unemployed. The official unemployment rate is given as 30%, where Johnson reckons this to have been 40% in 2015 – and it has only worsened. Given the current economic recession, it will soon be a lot higher and untenable. No wonder there are demonstrations on an almost daily basis, people dancing and singing and burning tyres. A few years ago, for the first time, I was concerned at a protest demonstration in our area, about 600 yards down the road from our home, burning and chanting, all the local shops were closed for fear of looting; this daylong demonstration took place outside the Walmer Police Station in PE, with the police taking no action. It remains common for local morning radio news reports on roads to be avoided because of burning tyres and protests turned violent. It is a pity everyone does not band together and march on the headquarters of the ANC namely Luthuli House and burn it down. This is unlikely to happen with the ANC firmly in control of the army and police, which they are still able to mobilise when they want. The lack of electricity and running water exacerbate the situation. This is the country in which South Africans now live thanks to the economic policies of the ANC and its total mismanagement of the economy including plundering state coffers along the way, a place where you cannot go for a walk along the beachfront, on a hiking or forest trail without doing so in fear of your life.

Chapter 7

Port Elizabeth – Then and Now

Port Elizabeth, my old hometown is a typical SA city and it is appropriate in the context of this book to compare it 27 years ago to today. The geographical boundaries of the city have hardly changed; there has been little outward expansion. In the old *white* areas, minimal upward development has taken place since 1994, with the majority of new homes being cluster housing or so-called townhouses – mainly due to safety concerns thanks to crime and the contraction of economic growth including the closure of major companies like General Motors and Ford. People feel a false sense of security in this type of housing but remain equally affected by crime. It may be noted here that for the past five years or more, annual car sales – a major economic barometer – have declined each year; in the first quarter of 2021 alone, the decline was 7% against the same period in 2020.

The western boundary of the city which should have been the growth point has hardly moved. On the eastern side which houses the black townships, numerous basic houses have been built by the government in terms of its RDP housing scheme but certainly not enough of them. Huge squatter camps have mushroomed and are ubiquitous – one only has to drive on the main road to Uitenhage to see these. In contrast, in upmarket Mill Park through which I had a memory lane drive in recent times, all the homes have electric fences, high walls, armed response security signs, palisade/electric/razor-wire fencing and steel electric gates, and many had vicious dogs on the properties. Even in the USA where most people own guns, houses generally have no boundary fences or walls and gardens stretch to the open road.

A closer examination of the city centre reveals the extent of the inner-city decay. The once-proud buildings which housed the business sector are dilapidated. The whole area has become a slum with drugs and gangs dominating. Rubbish is strewn everywhere. The beautiful Victorian buildings of that era have not been maintained and the statue of Queen Victoria has been vandalised. The ANC is determined to destroy all things colonial – refusing to recognise the country's history. A country that has no history has no future.

The Queen Victoria Stature outside the Public Library in Port Elizabeth (now Gqeberha).

The stature has been defaced several times in the "new South Africa".
[Ack. eNCA]

The business community has relocated to the suburbs, much the same way as happened in Johannesburg Central with the building of Sandton City. The only problem is that the mob tends to follow the money.

Grand old hotels The Campanile, The Red Lion, The King Edward, The Griffin, The Phoenix, The Victoria and The Markham have all closed. A friend of mine tried to revive the longstanding Grand Hotel but, unfortunately, it has now also closed its doors.

The King Edward Hotel completed in 1903 [photo ack. Trip.com] in its heyday.

I have fond memories as a former student of UPE, now Nelson Mandela Metropolitan University, with the annual Fundraising Rag, floats along the main street, the public gathered *en masse* in a festive spirit and people tossed donations for charity to the students. Sadly, since the new South Africa, this tradition has disappeared.

The skyline of the city has not changed in 27 years apart from one 20-storey BBE development hotel built on the beachfront in 2009 – further evidence of economic decline.

PE has been blessed with beautiful beaches but tragically they have become a dangerous place for taking a stroll alone – and a decidedly no-go area after dark. An effort was made to improve the beachfront area by building additional ponds and walkways – sadly now derelict with the pools lying empty and pipes hanging from the walls. PE once had a world-famous aquarium with dolphin shows attracting many thousands - sadly the dolphins are long gone and the vast seawater pool lies completely drained. A kiddies' miniature train once operated by Round Table has also closed. One of the biggest disappointments has been the demise of Happy Valley

53

which once displayed beautiful children's caricatures such as Snow White and the Seven Dwarfs, Jack and the Beanstalk, the Old Woman in the Shoe and many others lit up at night for a beautiful show, especially in the summer season. It attracted crowds of visitors but is now in ruins, following violent robberies and rapes.

The beachfront is always overrun on public holidays especially at Easter, Christmas and New Year when thousands from the black townships descend on the beaches. Tons of rubbish are left behind to be cleared the next day. The largely coloured community in the same way take over the public barbecue facilities (*braai*) situated at the end of the beach road. When this happens, the whites visit these areas at their peril. The Walmer (black squatter) township adjacent to the affluent suburb of Walmer has spread down to Summerstrand, the well-to-do beachfront area. This has resulted in a marked increase in crime and many people have moved away, citing that they felt like prisoners in their homes, more so on days when the beaches were invaded by hordes.

One of the major tourist attractions was the Apple Express, a narrow-gauge train that ran from the beachfront out to Hankey, a small town some 50 km inland. This daily trip ceased due to a lack of maintenance and funds. In years gone by, every September relay teams of athletes would race against the train, with many spectators lining the route. This major sponsored event disappeared from the calendar.

Fort Frederick, built by the British settlers on top of a hill overlooking Algoa Bay is now an eyesore inhabited by vagrants, stinks of excretion and piles of rubbish. Further up the road is St. George's Park where the famous cricket ground is housed. It contains well laid out gardens used by generations of people for relaxation but became a hotspot for criminals and vagrants; a palisade fence has been erected around its perimeter in an attempt to stem the tide. The war memorial in the park also needs restoration and maintenance. Nearby is the Baakens River Valley, a once-upon-a-time walking trail with multiple picnic spots along the way. This large valley divides the city in two and sadly, many people have been mugged, assaulted and women raped *in the valley*. This is now also a no-go area so much so the council has erected signs at the entrances warning people of the dangers and not to walk alone.

Another bone of contention is the removal of the oil storage tanks and iron-ore and coal dumps in the central harbour area which cause discolouration of all surrounding properties thanks to the city living up to its name as the windy city. Transnet, one of the SOEs agreed many years ago to move these structures to the Coega industrial zone (renamed The Port of Ngqura) west of the city but this has never been done due to lack of funds.

Yet another major attraction, the Campanile, a tower similar to the *Kampanile* in Venice, with its magnificent vistas of the city at its summit for those who are brave enough to climb its 204 steps, is in disuse. No doubt it is looked down on as a colonial memorial today situated in the wrong part of town next to the black taxi rank.

The Campanile, with acknowledgments to Nelson Mandela Bay Tourism

One achievement the ANC managed was to create the Red Location Museum in New Brighton Township, a memorial to the apartheid era, visited by many thousands of tourists. Even this is no longer in use because of a total lack of maintenance.

One of the city's two horse racing venues namely Arlington has closed and been converted to a low-cost housing development. Nearby, the Walmer Country Club which catered for golf, tennis, lawn bowls, swimming and squash was recently forced to close, mainly due to numerous attacks and robberies of players on the golf course, and the stoning of cars on the road to the club. It had become commonplace for golfers to carry firearms whenever they played the game. This land is earmarked for further expansion of the black township opposite, that is, when the city council finally pays the purchase price for the land, outstanding for over a decade.

To crown everything the Tourist Information Centre is no longer operating. This is nonsensical leading to the perception that the city is no longer a tourist destination.

Even the odd cruise liner which docks for the day does so only to enable passengers to visit the nearby game reserves to view the Big Five animals in the flesh.

The beautiful Victorian railway station in the centre of the city with its seven platforms is now only used by very few passenger trains and in need of serious renovation. The main library has been closed for 8-years for refurbishment but one now learns that after spending R21 million another R18 million is required to complete the job, quite clearly ludicrous (the funds being siphoned to cronies yet again). The public hospitals are in dire need of major facelifts and structural repair. Sandford Maternity Home behind the Provincial Hospital is completely derelict and was closed down. A few years ago, the city was awarded the National Swimming Championships but the main swimming bath stood empty and had to be refurbished at great cost to bring it up to standard. Whether the pools around the city have been emptied due to the drought or lack of maintenance is a moot question.

The St George's Park swimming pool today – acknowledgments to Herald Live

When driving from the city centre to North End every second shop is closed and rubbish is strewn all over the place. The council endeavours to clean the main street every week but it only takes a day to get back to where it was, as people simply throw their rubbish out of the taxis endlessly driving through red traffic lights chasing their next fare. Further out in the industrial area of Deal Party, most of the warehouses and manufacturing premises stand empty.

Very little road maintenance is done and motorists have to try and avoid the numerous potholes. Most of the road markings are no longer visible and weeds grow on the roads and pavements. Before departing SA, driving home from the golf club along Target Kloof one night, I counted that at least 50% of the street lights were not working.

PE is situated in a fairly dry rainfall area and the dams are at critically low levels with water restrictions in place for the last five years. There is plenty of water available. It only needs connecting a pipeline to the Orange River project. After more than 15 years there is still no end to the project in sight, despite Zuma's visit to PE some six years ago during a previous water crisis and his promise to immediately provide R400 million needed to complete this pipeline.

Meanwhile, millions of litres of water bypass PE and needlessly flow into the sea. A close relative worked at the Research Institute where the testing of the water was done and remarked she would not drink the local tap water.

In all major shopping centres around the country, there is the scourge of car guards, people who *look after* your car in return for a R5 tip. Failure to pay has often resulted in scratches or dents to the vehicle.

Gqeberha is the new official name of the city of Port Elizabeth much to the chagrin of many who are unable to pronounce its new name and find it totally unacceptable. The name Port Elizabeth was given to the city by the forefathers from the landing of the 1820 settlers in 1820 to the 1990s, and who built the city to what it is or should I say what it was a few decades ago. If ever the city wanted to promote tourism this certainly was not the way to go about things. Even forgetting the added attractions Cape Town has, if you were a potential tourist, how likely would you be to choose Gqeberha over Cape Town? One is reminded of the old quote by Sir Winston Churchill – A *nation that forgets its past has no future. Understanding that learning about your history is not about making any one person or people-group feel guilty. You cannot be guilty of actions that took place before you were born.*

This is very sage advice on which the ANC is either totally ignorant or simply ignores to promote its own agenda.

And the locals still claim it is a great city in which to live!

Chapter 8

The Judiciary and the Justice System

It would at this stage be remiss not to discuss the situation regarding the judicial system and here I include the various branches of criminal justice and private civil law.

The criminal justice section: by and large, the magistrates in the lower courts and the judges in the higher courts still appear to mete out justice in the cases before them. That is not to say I think that they are all competent. Under the affirmative action policies of the ANC over many years, most public service employees are incompetent. The simple fact is the government has not employed people on merit but only on colour (and on gender to provide a sprinkling of female jurors). Significantly, the country's top judges in the Constitutional Court and the Supreme Court of Appeal will soon all be black and typically they are paid top salaries, which continue when they retire. The problem with the criminal courts is the overload of cases, postponed at the drop of a hat. A lot of hardened criminals are granted bail rather than held in custody pending trial and, in many cases, commit more crimes while awaiting a court date. It often happens that the prosecution does not prepare properly for the trial, due to a lack of skills and after numerous postponements, magistrates simply strike the matter from the roll, the criminals free to carry on and plunder yet again. What also happens is that dockets go missing, sometimes with the help of corrupt police members, and the matter cannot proceed. Cash too often outweighs justice. One wonders who is paying who in such situations. The adage of *justice delayed is justice denied* is applicable in SA.

Even if there was a decent success rate with prosecutions, the government cannot cope with the number of prisoners it has to feed as the jails have remained overcrowded since 1993. Of course, the government, as with everything else, has not spent significantly on infrastructure including new prisons. It's hard to imagine a more serious crime than cold-blooded murder yet all the *normal* prisons are full of such worthless beings who are in any event entitled to parole consideration after 20 years despite a *life sentence*. A survey has shown that some 80% of the country's population would vote for the reimposition of the death penalty (repealed under the new Constitution), the murder rates have been so high. The Constitution focuses on citizens' *sanctity of life*, but life is cheaper in SA than anywhere in the world. Black township dwellers form street committees to take the law into their own hands. Vigilante groups beat people to death with fence wire or the (alleged) perpetrators are executed by necklacing, pouring petrol over them, placing a tyre over their head to lock their arms from escape and striking a match. What a way to go. Some feel it puts less strain on the judiciary. Then in the media, a top official will announce that the perpetrators will be pursued with the full might of the law but nothing ever happens. Maybe because the police get intimidated by threats of violence to their families which certainly does happen as one also reads about police being robbed of their guns and murdered. The fear of police entering any protest crowd is palpable.

One shudders to think about how many criminals go unpunished in SA with its hopelessly understaffed and ill-equipped police service. When robberies and theft occur the incident is simply recorded at the local police station if the complainant is lucky enough to have insurance cover and be compensated for their loss. A complainant went to the Humewood Police Station in PE to report the theft of a laptop PC from his car and, when he returned a week later to ask how far the police had progressed in their investigation, he was met with a blank stare and stony silence. The primary reason for reporting the matter is for the insurance claim, not in the hope the police will do anything to investigate the crime. When an occasional arrest is made the media is sure to make a meal of it. It would be interesting to know what percentage of cases are not even investigated given the lack of skills, facilities and qualified manpower. A good guess is most are just archived. The rights of criminals are perceived as more protected than the innocent people who bear the brunt of their frequently savage violence and general criminality.

When President Cyril Ramaphosa took over in 2018, he got rid of the boss of the National Prosecuting Authority (NPA) and the new appointee made an amazing speech about how she was going to prosecute all and sundry, especially high-profile government criminals. I think that was the last heard from her.

The government of the day keenly appoints commissions of enquiry into wrongdoings when they are exposed by the media, more as a diversionary tactic than anything. The corrupt mega-billion arms deal during the presidency of Mandela and more recently the Zondo Commission into so-called *state capture* by the Guptas and Zuma at the helm, are examples. The Zondo Commission also seems to be going nowhere. How the judiciary and the NPA allow the likes of Zuma to evade justice all these years is incredible. Zuma has openly flaunted his refusal to appear before this Commission. No warrant for his arrest has been issued, standard procedure for any other citizen, and he even had the Minister of Police Bheki Cele visiting him for tea (while in contempt of the Commission), and the two of them posed for smiling photos afterwards. Zuma threatened on record to spill the beans on the corruption of others and not *go down alone*, so it seems he is untouchable.

In recent times there was a double murder of two elderly ladies in their late 80s in a supposedly secure PE retirement village despite all the latest security systems. A robbery turned into their horrific deaths by strangulation. Of course, no arrests have been made despite establishing it was an inside job. An interesting side issue is that the officer who was first on the scene is the son in law of my family friend living in the UK. After this gruesome finding, it was enough to tip him over the edge and he now has migrated to the UK.

While still on the subject of the criminal judiciary it would not go amiss to mention the Oscar Pistorius *blade-runners* trial. Broadcast around the world on live TV and presided over by, in my opinion, a black lady judge who appeared to be out of her depth; she rejected the evidence of witnesses who came to the court of their own free volition and testified that they heard a terrified woman screaming at the top of her voice followed by the gunshots in the dead of the night. The mind boggles. And then, she also made an incorrect finding that he was only guilty of culpable homicide and not murder, which was overturned on appeal by the state. Of course, Oscar and his uncle threw a huge amount of money at his defence. The net result was he still saved a few extra years' jail time.

Reverting to the private civil law segment of the judiciary, matters dealing with money claims, divorces and the like, I had more to do with these and had very little criminal law experience. As more and more black people were appointed to the judiciary, in my experience the standards dropped.

I was involved in a case where a black client sued me for professional negligence in paying out money to an estate agent in a property transaction. After the hearing, we eventually received the magistrate's judgment a few months later. Yes, it went against me, and as advised by my counsel we appealed. The indecipherable language used by the magistrate was so atrocious it was difficult to decipher what he tried to convey. We had to obtain a copy of the whole record of the case for the appeal but this was never forthcoming from the state. The matter died a natural death.

In 1999 I received instructions from my friend, a top insurance broker, to institute proceedings against Sanlam Insurance and ABSA Bank in respect of various insurance policies which the companies refused to pay out in respect of his eyesight disability claim. He was the number one broker in the country while in the employ of ABSA Insurance Brokers in 1995 and as his eyes deteriorated, he had to employ an additional secretary who would fill in the application forms for him as he could no longer read the

63

small print. One of his superiors would not accept this and he was eventually medically boarded due to this disability. In pursuing his claims, we had the services of a senior advocate and myself who agreed to act on the basis that we would receive double the normal fees, by then an acceptable *no win no fee* agreement. From my point of view, this seemed like a really good deal with strong merits in the client's favour, as the policies were up to date and his claim was covered. Of course, the insurance companies defended the cases through Werksmans, one of the top corporate law firms from Johannesburg. We had spent many hours studying the documents and we were happy with the merits of our case. Soon after the matter commenced a senior advocate from Johannesburg flew down with his instructing attorney and we had a round table conference at the office of the insurer's local attorneys. We were told: *This is not a case you can win,* to which we replied that we would see them in court. We had numerous consultations with expert medical witnesses and the other witnesses close to the case and we were well prepared for all eventualities but not for what followed. The opposition filed what is known as a special plea in which various technical defences were raised. One of them was that the companies had separate entities which dealt with the vast pool of client funds and therefore we had sued the wrong companies. Ludicrous, given the fact the original policies stated quite clearly the contract was between the insurers and the client. In any event, the special plea hearing is held before the main trial. The defendants sent the costliest advocates to argue the matter for them. The judge assigned to the case was a judge of colour who had been fast-tracked to the bench despite a marked lack of experience. I recall when this judge was in private practice that he hardly ever received any briefs from attorneys – on whom advocates solely depend for work – and certainly there were no important cases. When we eventually received a written judgment some three months later it naturally went against us. In the meantime, it occurred to me the judge was so out of his depth he could not grasp what was going on, given the technical arguments by the upcountry legal team. Their bullying tactics swayed the judge. Naturally, we decided to appeal and it was agreed the matter should be heard in the Supreme Court of Appeal in Bloemfontein, the judicial capital of the country, rather than first appeal to the High Court in Grahamstown which headed the Provincial Division. The thinking was that whoever won there would appeal to the Supreme Court of Appeal regardless of the outcome in the lower court. However, before following that route leave to appeal must first be granted by the judge who heard the case. Lo and behold, after a further court appearance and additional costs being incurred, to our amazement, the judge refused leave to appeal. When a judge makes such a ruling, he has to be convinced that no higher court can come to a different conclusion; this was not the situation in our case. We were all dumbfounded, maybe even the opposition was too. In my opinion, the judge did not want his judgment scrutinised by more senior judges on appeal. The only option left to our client was to petition the Supreme Court of Appeal for permission to appeal. The procedure is that a judge sits in his Chambers in Bloemfontein with a pile of petitions to read through. He then decides on his own whether or not to allow the matter to be appealed before a standard bench of five judges. One imagines that if overloaded with work, the judge simply stamps this as disapproved. I am not suggesting this is what happened in our case but the outcome was the same. We were denied our right to appeal, and that was the end of the matter. We had lost through a technicality and as far as I am concerned the judicial system failed my client. I have since been reliably told the Supreme Court of Appeal only grants a very small number of the thousands of petitions for leave to appeal lodged each year. I do not know what the Johannesburg attorneys knew that I did not know but this experience certainly proves the truism that money can buy justice. The defendants were awarded their costs and after 5 years of litigation, their bill amounted to almost R1 million. When our client refused to pay they duly sent the sheriff around but there were no assets and no money to satisfy the writ of execution. The client had the consolation it cost defendants more than this but it was still a win for them as the claims amounted to at least R3 million.

The Supreme Court of Appeal, Bloemfontein

I should also mention I had a colleague who years ago employed a black articled clerk to enable him to qualify as an attorney. Within a year or two of qualifying, he was suddenly appointed as a High Court judge and had a meteoric rise to the Supreme Court of Appeal which would normally have taken many years to achieve. I have heard he is a competent judge today, perhaps a *lucky* appointment under the policy of affirmative action but I question what the position might have been if this was not so. Well, the simple answer to that is even if such a decision was wrong it would not have made any difference as a judge is appointed for life and can only be removed for acts of impropriety.

As far back as 2004, Jeremy Gauntlett and the Cape Town Bar Association tried to have the Judge President of the Western Cape John Hlophe removed from office for alleged political interference in a Constitutional Court matter involving none other than Jacob Zuma. Hlophe is a controversial figure for the number of allegations of impropriety levelled against him that have damaged the credibility of the justice system – to the extent it existed in the first place. After many years of litigation, the matter stalled as the original complainants, namely some Constitutional Court judges, were no longer prepared to comment, plus Hlophe wanted to appeal the decision to the Constitutional Court, and this posed a constitutional crisis since excluding the complainant judges meant the court could not raise the required forum of eleven judges. One wonders what went on behind the scenes. When the country's top advocates lead the charge, you may be pretty certain they have all their ducks in a row. After Zuma announced his nomination of Sandile Ngcobo as South Africa's next Chief Justice, Hlophe admitted his decision to side with Zuma had been his undoing. In September 2009, Hlophe received permission from the Justice Ministry to return to work as Judge President. In 2021, the Judicial Services Commission (JSC) belatedly made a finding that Hlophe was indeed guilty of *gross misconduct*. True to form, Hlophe has not resigned and intends to pursue his last right of appeal. Even if he fails in his appeal, Parliament still has to vote on his impeachment and removal, for which a two-thirds majority is required. Before that stage, Hlophe will have reached the mandatory retirement age for all judges of 70 years. Amazingly, he continues to serve on the Commission to appoint new judges in the Western Cape.

About 10 years ago I had an interesting chance encounter with a man who joined us to make up a four-ball at the upmarket Houghton Golf Club in Johannesburg on the newly-designed Jack Nicklaus golf course. A good friend and I used to travel to Johannesburg over the Easter long weekend and stay with his son. Our fourth golfer after the game related to us over a drink that he spent 3 months of the year with his elderly mother in Houghton and the remainder of the year between his villa in Spain and his home in the UK. He is an IT guru and in the 1990s he had the sole agency to sell Microsoft software in SA. He made a tidy sum but then was side-lined and lost his subsequent legal battles against Microsoft. He told how he sued a big bank and became convinced one of the judges had been bribed as he thought he had a cast-iron case. His conclusion: it is foolhardy to take on the major banks or insurance companies as you cannot win – similar to my sentiments above. However, his story did have a happy ending as he subsequently wrote a software package for medical practices and had some 2000 doctors on his books, enabling him to lead his current lifestyle.

The militant Julius Malema, head of the EFF and arch racist, is the chairperson of the JSC and has delighted in what can only be described as the *flagellation* of any white judicial candidates, which included in 2021 overlooking as Constitutional Court judges, Sutherland and Unterhalter, widely regarded as the best legal brains in the country, purely because they were not black.

The last story to relate regarding the judiciary is The State vs David Price, who I knew very well for many years. He was an articled clerk at the same time as me, then a colleague for some 25 years. In all my dealings with him, I always found him to be a person of integrity. What happened to him was a travesty of justice and a whole book should be written about his experiences. I paraphrase what happened in his encounter with the SA judicial system. A successful attorney and even more so as an investment broker, he fell into a trap when he was called by a client to confirm a cheque deposited into his firm's trust account, saying instructions would follow as the funds were (supposedly) earmarked for a commercial property purchase. Some ten days later the *client* again called him to say the property deal had fallen through and requested a refund. A crossed "not-transferable" cheque was issued to the client's corporation. Unknown to Price, almost a year later it emerged the original cheque had been stolen. He was charged with fraud, along with the two actual perpetrators. He was very well off financially at the time, mortgage-free and debt-free and certainly did not need money. Another attorney who had experienced the same deposit scenario above, before any fraud could take place then, under pressure from the police and to avoid prosecution himself, turned state witness against Price. The local prosecuting authority informed Price and his then-attorney, Belinda Hartle, who subsequently became an advocate and is today a judge of the High Court, that there was no case against him and the prosecution docket would be closed. A couple of weeks later, Price and his attorney, Hartle, were again called by the same local prosecutor and informed there was *political pressure* for Price to be prosecuted. I must mention that less than four years before his arrest in 1999 before all this happened, he had set up successful branches of his practice in East London and King William's Town, the seat of the property deeds registry for the part of the province. In doing so and by providing superior service, he had taken away a lot of work from the attorneys of the region and this incensed them. In particular, one senior attorney from King William's Town even threatened to have him *taken down*. What transpired was that the Attorney General (AG) at the time a certain Les Roberts was a good friend of this senior King William's Town attorney and the AG had also worked with Judge Jansen who was appointed to hear the trial of David Price. They say it is a small world but a few years later I did some legal work for a client who had divorced his wife and she subsequently married Jansen. However, she had stolen R1 million from her previous husband's business and he laid a criminal charge against her in 1998, apart from a second charge of fraud and theft of another R200,000 laid by her subsequent employer in 1999 – neither of which were ever finally investigated, even after the docket went back and forth and eventually landed in the National Director of Public Prosecutions office in Pretoria, headline news in the Weekend Post in May 2002. And so, securing the conviction of David Price would make everyone happy. Even the attorney(s) in King William's Town. The trial went ahead and eventually, Price was convicted in the year 2000. In arriving at his guilty finding this same judge stated in his written judgment, therefore a matter of record, that he preferred the state's evidence on a *balance of probabilities* – a principle only supposed to apply in a civil action. Most of us, even non-lawyers, know, in a criminal trial the accused must be found guilty *beyond all reasonable doubt*, a heavy onus placed squarely on the state. All said and done, Les Roberts got his conviction which, by the way, he heralded in his retirement speech as one of his major career achievements. The judge's wife was never prosecuted and the King William's Town and East London attorneys got back to their lazy-business styles again. David Price's attorney had a conversation (which Price also overheard) with a senior advocate whose late father had been a judge, while his case was still in progress, confirming the above collusion. The judge sentenced Price to 15 years' imprisonment stating this was the prescribed minimum sentence, although shortly thereafter the SCA passed a decision that confirmed a lesser sentence was in order if the minimum sentence was disproportionate; Jansen had said were it not for the minimum sentence he would have imposed 7 years on Price. It is worth pointing out that the actual monetary loss, in this case, was R325,000 (or about £16,000 at current exchange rates), and that Price's gain was zero, removing any motive. The same judge refused leave to appeal against his conviction and also refused bail pending a petition for leave to appeal. That is not the end of the story as David Price went through the whole appeal system right through to the Constitutional Court (twice) in endeavours to prove his innocence. After his case, he managed to find new evidence including that the police had deliberately tampered with a videotape recorded by the police – which Price said proved his innocence – to render the recording "snowy" and remove the sound, but the Constitutional Court had already ruled against him previously and was not prepared to entertain any further representations. The later forensic analysis of this video showed perfect sound and picture at the beginning and end, except for the middle section featuring Price. Unlike any ANC cadres or persons with celeb status being heard before the full bench of nine Constitutional Court judges, Price was not given a hearing of any kind in either of his Constitutional Court applications. These were dismissed on the papers alone by a single Constitutional Court judge. The net result was that he spent just less than 6 years in prison and that's another whole story on its own. Contrary to popular belief, that was not the end of his story. Price was not *free* but under strict parole conditions until 2012 when, finally, his nightmare was over. Even today people continue to judge him as a fraudster. From what I have discussed it should be clear I do not believe the judiciary is all that it is made out to be. In times of crisis which I think are inevitable given the economic trend, I would not rely too heavily on the judiciary to be the guardian angel of SA citizens. We have seen what happened in Zimbabwe when the judiciary bows to the wishes of the politicians. We have also noted that public sector pay in SA is much higher than in the private sector. Similar to the health sector, what lawyer would not want to be a judge and get paid a fortune, have set work hours, not have to worry about the costs of running a practice or from where the next case will come. And at the end of the day on retirement, have a fantastic pension for life not having to make any provision for retirement. With affirmative action policies, most of the top legal brains such as there are left in the country are not used or have emigrated.

I have a friend who was a top advocate but emigrated two years ago after becoming frustrated with the judiciary. He has since gone into mediation which has become very popular, particularly in SA, because litigants have learned the perils of finding *justice* in the courts. I once heard a colleague remark before a court case that it was heads or tails considering the presiding officer appointed – even though he felt he had an open and shut case. Johnson in his 2015 book also expressed concern about the judiciary saying it has been *trashed*, and after all, does not have the executive power to enforce its judgments even if they are good ones.

Chapter 9

The Constitution

As we have seen, South Africa's Constitution was drafted when Codesa was set up in the early 1990s and later hailed as being modern, progressive and one of the best in the world. As Johnson showed, minority interests were only protected on the aspect of land ownership. However, to change the Constitution merely required a two-thirds majority vote by the government of the day. Given SA's demographic makeup and blind allegiance by the masses to the ANC, there was only ever going to be one party in power for many years to come. The ANC triumphantly proclaimed its liberation of the people. Zuma made his infamous assertion that the ANC would remain in power *until Jesus returns* – we all pray this soon happens. In the early days of its rule, the ANC could have changed the Constitution regarding the land ownership rule but there was no need to do so at the time and of course, it would have been too early to contemplate such a move; in any event, this risked the anger of the outside world. The ANC has since lost its two-thirds majority but in the last election, it still had 57% of the popular vote despite leading the country on the road to ruin. The EFF gained almost 12% of the vote so the populist left in a coalition government would quite easily be able to *bend* the Constitution to its will. But this does not seem to be necessary. At the ANC's conference two years ago President Ramaphosa promptly announced the government was going to push ahead with land reform (whatever that means, but including land expropriation without compensation). If you own a palatial home in Camps Bay, or perhaps a wine farm which some politician fancies for himself, is this up for grabs? Since then, the matter has been at the forefront of its to-do list while being egged on by Julius Malema and his cohorts. A draft bill was drawn up and tabled in Parliament. It gives wide-ranging powers but does not specify in detail exactly what and how much land is involved. It is supposedly restricted to agricultural land only but the unthinkable question is: does it include urban land and thereby threaten the country's whole deeds registration system which has been entrenched for centuries? I remember, in my early days when studying to become a conveyancer, perusing some of the old deeds in the *dungeons* of the original Cape Town Deeds Office going back to the 1700s. The property conveyancing handbook by Jones proudly extolled the security of property tenure and excellence of the deeds registration system in SA, hailed as an example for many first world countries. In my visits to the Cape Town Deeds Office as a lawyer, I recall the old land deeds signed by various Registrars in bygone times, their flowery calligraphic signatures accompanied by flourishes that occupied half a page. Institutions such as Afriforum and the opposition parties will decidedly take the government to court as these proposed changes are contrary to the Constitution. It appears there is a devious scheme to circumvent the Constitution through legislation rather than amending the Constitution. The whole saga may take a long time to play out but, in the end, there is no doubt in my mind the government will get its way whether it does so illegally or with the help of the EFF. Johnson demonstrated that if SA heads down the Zimbabwean route, land expropriation is inevitable and will have disastrous effects on the country.

As far as agricultural land goes, there have been noises made that white farmers have lots of unused lands and could quite easily give up half of them. Whether this is true or not I do not know, but what black people would do with such land is a matter of record. Blacks given land have almost without exception shown they are not farmers and do not have the skills to make a go of it. Even some of the black elite who acquired farms have been unable to succeed. Certainly, the white farmers would not give of their time, skills and resources to assist them. Their personal and financial responsibilities aside, the fact is they have been violently targeted through what seems to be orchestrated attacks over many years without any sympathy, recognition of, or action to tackle farm murders on the part of the government. Statistics confirm it is exceedingly dangerous to be a farmer, black or white, in SA.

There are major concerns about the sustainability of food production. A last major point by Johnson was the majority of blacks are now urbanised and would not have a clue what to do with farmland or a return to subsistence farming to feed themselves. The ANC is only pushing ahead under the guise of *economic transformation* to further enrich the top cadres with its empty promises of employment for the masses. Coming back to SA's *wonderful* Constitution, it is unlikely any part of this will help the masses, due to the ANC-elites' iron-grip on power. After all, with physical control of the army and the police, they can do as they please. A cadre lucky enough to have a job and even more so an overpaid one will certainly toe the line. The vast majority of African countries and their dictators as perfect examples of how Western democracy has no chance in Africa. SA looks to be no exception. Johnson mentioned vote-rigging had already taken place. Evidence of this in the last election was the tampering with many ballot boxes. The result is the ANC is unlikely to ever lose an election whether by fair means or foul. As Johnson suggested, it will never give up power and has the means to enforce this. The ANC cannot afford to allow this to happen. Imagine an opposition party like the DA one day coming into power and discovering the way the country's coffers have been plundered over the years. There would not be enough jails in all of Africa to house all the guilty ANC cadres.

One of the few saving features of SA's Constitution which Johnson saw as a positive is that there have (now) been five black presidents since 1994. On this point, I disagree. The priority of the ANC top echelons is simply being able to join all the other pigs feeding at the same trough – in line with *Animal Farm* by George Orwell – and it does not matter whether a dictator acts alone or shares the leadership. The ANC has always used *collective decisions,* a clever way of avoiding any individual responsibility or liability.

Pre-1994, SA was a modern industrial country with advanced infrastructure and run on capitalist principles. This had to continue to improve the wellbeing of the masses and lift them out of poverty which sadly has not happened. As Johnson said, the whole hierarchy of the ANC was indoctrinated in the beliefs of socialism and communism from an early age and cannot be persuaded otherwise because it is so ingrained and was adopted as the ANC's official policy in 1969.

From Russia to modern-day Venezuela communism and socialism just do not work. I thought Kgalema Motlanthe, the short-term president, was more enlightened until I discovered he is a staunch socialist.

Secondly, it has been argued that no more could have been done to draft a better or more fool-proof Constitution to protect the rights of all the citizens. However, to follow through with the modern capitalist way of doing things and thereby drive the economy, provide jobs and a decent standard of living for all, the principle of merit should have been enshrined in the Constitution to prevent the ANC's self-destructive path of affirmative action. A major flaw in the Constitution was that it did not outlaw communism/socialism, factors that would never have led to the handing over of power by the Nationalist government, had it been aware of the ANC's long-term agenda to espouse both these policies. In comparison, India and Malaysia have uplifted many millions of their citizens through better education and skills provision, in the process preventing the need for extreme socialism as has happened in SA. The economy could have grown at a fantastic rate with productivity at all-time record levels. As people achieve better education and skills' levels they would evolve into the system. There would be plenty of jobs in the long run and unemployment would be at around 5% instead of the existing dangerous 40% situation (pre-Covid).

I must mention an elderly PE attorney who formed a political party known as the Merit Party. Sol Schkolne was quite a character and in the late 1980s and early 1990s, we would often chat at the local deeds office for blacks which catered for 99-year lease transactions and was disbanded when full property rights were granted to all blacks. Politics was on everyone's mind and he would bend the ears of anyone happy to listen. He published a book on the subject of meritocracy being the yardstick for every aspect of life. Unfortunately, not enough people took him up on his theories and his party fell away after failing to gain any representation.

The DA once had merit as its core value but has since changed its tune, although still not in favour of affirmative action. The argument for BEE is the redress of past wrongs. The problem in practice has been cronyism and the employment of blacks unqualified to handle their job responsibilities. People thrust into top positions in the new government since 1994 have been hopelessly under-educated and not up to the task. The same applies to the whole of the public sector and the only qualification was to be a well-connected card-carrying member of the party.

A classic example of failed BEE policy is the Denau Prime Grape Farm, which once produced 30,000 to 40,000 boxes of export grapes, and now lies in ruins; the workers made shareholders under BEE kept declaring dividends to themselves until the farm was bankrupt – despite a non-repayable grant of R2 million from the provincial government and a loan facility of R800,000 from a bank which remains unpaid.

Denau Prime Grape Farm

Thirdly, the Afrikaner population seems to have lost its historical spirit to honour the covenant undertaken by the Boer Voortrekkers, the spirit to fight for their rights and their very identity. Afrikaans is spoken in no other country. The annual Day of the Covenant was changed to the Day of Reconciliation. Stellenbosch University, long regarded as a bastion of Afrikaner nationalism incredibly no longer boasts Afrikaans as its language of tuition. There is no longer the unity once found among nationalist Afrikaner people, including among farmers scattered across the country. During the Boer War which ended in 1902, a similar thing happened when the farmers in the Cape refused to get involved in supporting their brothers up north.

Fourthly, an extremely important thing never taken care of was the vital need for a decent education system for a successful SA. Not only would this have prevented the brain drain but a new highly skilled labour force would have emerged and eliminated the need to import skills such as in the medical and engineering fields. SA has a total of just 26 universities including technical colleges, compared to the UK with a similar population which has 106 universities. The

77

failed SA Education Department has resulted in fewer children attending school and more roaming the streets begging. And this all happens while the population explodes. A straightforward one-man-one-vote was never going to work according to Western democracy standards. Instead of wasting time and money dwelling on the past such as the Truth and Reconciliation Commission, a line should have been drawn in the sand to let bygones be bygones. Instead, the ANC has embarked on a policy of revenge despite the Constitution which is largely ignored and is doing its utmost to destroy the country. The bottom line of any revolution is to destroy the existing and replace this with a new order. Many blacks still see Mandela as a sell-out to the whites for reaching a negotiated settlement at Codesa; this was not what they wanted. They wanted – and some would justifiably argue, still want – a revolution. The only time the Constitution is questioned these days is when someone tries to take a civil matter to the Constitutional Court by finding some loophole whereby one's constitutional rights have been infringed. It is (incorrectly) used as an additional court of appeal. The taxing question is if the Constitution will stand the test of time, as there are already signs of it being ignored and if not, then tailored to suit specific needs?

My conclusion is that the Constitution was not suited to the new South Africa.

Chapter 10

The Banks

It has often been said by many observers that SA is on par with the most modern banking systems in the world. Therefore, it should theoretically be able to look after what was once a first-world economy, except that this has since degenerated into at least a third world country and some people even joke now a *fifth-world* country.

Yet, a closer examination shows for banks to thrive they need enough decent customers to make a profit. As I put pen to paper, the SA economy is in recession (officially, two quarters of negative growth) and the outlook is very bleak given the ANC's chosen path.

SA has four major banks namely Standard, ABSA, First National and Nedbank. More recently, Capitec Bank has emerged, targeting the lower end of the market, granting loans to all and sundry without any tangible security. The only requirement was a payslip showing regular employment and this was mostly applicable to those in secure government jobs. I'm able to attest to this, having had many property transactions at the lower end of the market where the majority of buyers were Capitec clients. This bank lent them R100,000 to R200,000 and would not register a bond over the property as security. To my mind, this is not sound banking practice, more so with the economy contracting and the government's finances deteriorating. There is already talk of cutting back on the public service wage bill whether it be by retrenchment or actual wage cuts. However, before this can happen the ANC will have to deal with the mighty trade unions. But the government cannot afford to continue paying more than 40% of fiscal income on salaries. This does not augur well for Capitec let alone the other major banks. A short time ago there was concern in the market that Capitec's bad debts were getting out of hand and its share price dropped. It was able to reassure the market all was well but the question is for how long? Inevitably, the other banks will also be under pressure although their business interests are no longer confined to SA with overseas listings, particularly on the London Stock Exchange (LSE).

One thinks of Investec Bank which caters for the upper end of the market, and is listed on the LSE and operates from London. This bank sponsors England's international cricket team. Most of the banks will likely be alright in the long run but to what extent they will still operate in SA is an open question.

All SA banks have in recent times been restructuring and retrenching staff. A side issue here is the wide disparity between what the top executives pay themselves as opposed to the lowest-paid employees. In the case of Nedbank, in 2018/19 the CEO was paid R56 million with bonuses, whereas at the bottom of the rung it is a tiny fraction. This smacks of lopsided capitalism. Nedbank has appointed a board director who can only be described as a socialist, in 1997 he was adviser to the government on its BEE policies, with his directorship of Nedbank obviously as a reward.

Another question is how on earth the Guptas and Zuma managed to transfer so many billions of Rands offshore without the express complicity of the banks involved, including the Reserve Bank?

A recent example of such complicity has been ABSA Bank's denial of banking facilities to an individual simply because he was associated with the *Suidlanders* group, which is opposed to the ANC's policies.

The EFF has called for the nationalisation of the banks, amid a growing lobby for 51% black ownership. The SA Reserve Bank may be nationalised in 2021, thanks to a Bill introduced by none other than EFF leader, Julius Malema. Nationalisation can only be to cover up all the corrupt transactions sanctioned by the Reserve

Bank.

Unlike UK banks, the SA banks practise giant rip-offs in terms of customer fees for every facet of personal banking, which include cash deposit fees, cash withdrawal fees, monthly service fees, cheque book fees, administration fees, overdraft availability fees, not to mention usurious interest rates and penalties.

In line with all big public companies in SA, the banks have indulged in tokenism when it comes to complying with affirmative action policies, including some directors whose *contribution* is highly debatable.

Meanwhile, the banks and insurance maintain a firm grip on their control of the country.

Chapter 11

Corruption

The subject of corruption has been discussed many times earlier and Johnson mentioned many examples in his book.

One he cited concerned the Mining Charter, which stands out to me as the most mind-boggling. The Minister of Mineral Resources has the sole right to grant prospecting rights to mining companies. However, when given to favoured political and family friends in preference over an existing company already operating there, this creates a major problem. The *interloper* as he describes the newcomer(s) is then booted out at great expense by the original mineral-rights licence holder so it can continue with its mining operations. The interloper will typically receive a payout of around R10 million to "get rid of him".

Enquiries to the department are ignored. No wonder the leading mining companies have had enough. What a scam! As he points out all the top government ministers are only there to milk the system with impunity and not to do an actual job of work for the benefit of the people.

The huge ministerial pay package is not enough. When Zuma became president, his remuneration was in the order of R1.2 million; nine years later this was R3.4 million and Cabinet Ministers were paid R2.7 million, excluding *expenses*. The UK Prime Minister's yearly salary is 5 times the national average income, whereas the incumbent SA President, Ramaphosa's, is 19 times the national average and one of the highest presidential salaries in the world.

Anyone who has not read *The President's Keepers* by Jacques

Paauw should do so to gain more insight into the grand scale of corruption and theft. The book is mainly about how Zuma has managed to avoid prosecution and stay out of jail, but the examples set out are also mind-blowing, particularly Zuma's involvement with the Guptas, never mind the whole Nkandla debacle in which at least R250 million taxpayers' money was spent on Zuma's private compound, for improvements worth only about R20 million. In January 2018 the Zondo Commission of Enquiry was set up but, as with all of the other commissions of enquiry, no finality is ever reached.

One of the main Zondo Commission witnesses provided a video of the late Gavin Watson paying out one million rand bundles of notes destined for Zuma's pocket in return for lucrative government contracts. Watson died in suspicious circumstances in a road accident. Just how much Zuma and his son and cohorts have extracted from corrupt dealings is not clear. What we do know is the Zumas have substantial properties in the UAE, courtesy of the Guptas. One can only guess at the value of balances in offshore bank accounts. He still enjoys a presidential pension for life! And of course, Zuma is immune to prosecution having the ANC and possibly the legal system on his side, His power base in Kwazulu-Natal province is still intact despite being supposedly in disgrace after being recalled by the party.

I liken him to a modern-day Dingaan, the ancient Zulu chief who was master of all he surveyed.

The likes of David Mabuza and Ace Magashule, now numbers 2 and 3 in the hierarchy of the ANC, are known for massive corruption while Premiers of their Provinces during Zuma's tenure. A whole book titled *The Gangster State* by Pieter-Louis Myburgh, a SA investigative journalist, published in 2019 set out all Magashule's wrongdoings yet he remains the party number 3. He is known as *the 10% man* demanding this amount on every deal where he has bestowed favours. He is one of the untouchables with a huge power base. One wonders how many security guards he or more probably the State employs to protect him. The same applies to David Mabuza who was guaranteed the vice presidency in return for allowing Ramaphosa to become president. Only Magashule is being prosecuted but he remains *innocent until proven guilty* and is emulating Zuma in avoiding his day in court. Ramaphosa had Jessie Duarte address a letter in May 2021 to Magashule, her immediate superior, confirming that Magashule has been suspended pending the outcome of his prosecution – on full pay of R133,000 per month – from his office as Secretary-General of the ANC.

The EFF Party Leader, Julius Malema, while leading the ANC Youth League, was also involved in substantial corruption in the Limpopo Province. The powers that be made some effort to claim unpaid taxes by attaching a property that he could only have acquired by illegal means. He also seems immune to prosecution, no doubt because the ANC is scared of him.

When you analyse the man at the helm, Ramaphosa, it is difficult to pinpoint nefarious dealings he may or not have had. Suffice it to say that he formed the NUMSA Trade Union in 1985 – which has since discredited him for the Marikana protest in 2012 which left 34 black miners shot dead by police, many shot in the back (after the police were authorised by Ramaphosa, in his capacity as an Anglo Platinum director and shareholder at that time, to use live ammunition) – and was a co-founder of SADTU, at which time he was not a man of means. As we know, Union bosses have coined it over decades, whether legally or otherwise.

Around 1996, I remember reading a Financial Mail article that stated Ramaphosa's dividends for the year from his shareholdings in Anglo-American totalled about R35 million, making him a billionaire. This begs the question of how he acquired the shares in the first place? We know that he was one of the favoured few when the ANC took over. His business interests such as McDonald's and Lonmin are well-documented but how did he acquire the capital to do so in the first place? As at January 2021, Ramaphosa is by far the wealthiest politician in SA at US$700 million net worth, with the next in line way below him, Mosima Gabriel at $200 million, Zuma at $20 million and Thabo Mbeki at $10 million. In 2012, Cyril Ramaphosa was made chairperson and a non-executive director of Optimum coal mine. Ramaphosa was the black economic empowerment partner for Glencore International which owned 68% of the shares in Optimum, SA's 6th-largest producer and 4th-largest exporter of coal. While Ramaphosa disinvested from his business interests to avoid his political conflict of interest, the Zondo Commission has heard Eskom arranged to pay R1,8 billion to Optimum, with former Eskom CEO alleging this was done under pressure from Ramaphosa. Most importantly, Ramaphosa is alleged to have influenced the price increase of coal supplied to Eskom, from R1, 500 to R4,500 per ton. And why did Ramaphosa just sit, watch and do nothing as number 2 in the party during Zuma's 9-year presidency, while all and sundry around him kept plundering the state coffers?

In contrast, since the election of the first President of the USA in 1776, the only billionaire president in its history, either before or after his term in office, has been Donald Trump.

According to reliable sources, Tokyo Sexwale, another ANC *fat cat* and former provincial premier and cabinet minister, acquired his wealth by the grant of a R20 million unsecured bank loan with which he bought Anglo American shares; these shot up in price at the time, and he sold them for R100 million, getting him off to a nice start. I had no such luck with my bank manager.

Let's not forget about the hundreds of billions lost to the ANC top brass over the years; one cannot even begin to guess how much has gone down the corruption drain lower down the chain - smaller amounts but by so many more people, from town mayors to the local police constable, adding up to who knows what.

In my property transfer law practice, a clearance certificate that all municipal service taxes have been paid is a prerequisite to registering the property transfer. In the black townships, there is a culture of non-payment and entitlement to free services. However, when you are unemployed it is a no-brainer that you do not pay. When the municipality finally takes action against someone the amount owing is so large that the owner might sell the property to pay the municipal arrears and hopefully pocket the difference just to survive. I have seen many accounts of over R100,000! What often happens is the agent in the deal has a contact at the municipality who will, for example, for a R2,000 bribe reduce the say R40,000 owing to R10,000, with this paid out of the purchase price. No wonder local municipalities are on their knees financially throughout the country.

A golfer I know related to me the saga when he applied for permission to operate a restaurant in an upmarket suburb. About a day or two before the council's meeting to decide the issue he received an anonymous call advising that if he deposited R30,000 into a certain account this would ensure the application was approved. He declined to take this gentleman, or should I say rogue, up on his offer and inevitably the application was declined.

Another property owner had trouble with the municipality because he paved his verge after removing the grass to provide extra parking for his business. It was reported in the local newspaper. A certain councillor was seen leaving the premises and suddenly the whole problem went away.

It is well known that many *tenderpreneurs* have enriched themselves through the award of government tenders to a favoured person despite higher tenders made, and to someone who does not have the skills to complete the project without comebacks. This often happened when RDP houses were built for the poor, the tender award invariably subject to a backhander. One day I was talking to my banker about a lady who had opened a new bank account for a company she had formed to get into the house-building business. The only problem was that she was employed by the municipality. If ever there was a conflict of interest! I would not be surprised if she was also one of the people responsible for awarding the tender contracts.

A client told me he knew someone who was involved in road construction in the north of the country and related how when he tendered for a R15 million contract to repair a stretch of road he was told to pay R250,000 into an anonymous bank account to secure the business. I do not know how that story ended.

The systemic problem is that corruption is so entrenched, with few, if any, prosecuted unless the media happens to get proof of underhand dealings and the government wants to be seen to do something about it. These are the very few unlucky sacrificial lambs or scapegoats to appease the public, and promote the idea that justice is not only done, but seen to be done.

Schabir Shaik, Jacob Zuma's *financial adviser* was convicted by Judge Squires – who named Zuma as the other party involved – of corruption and fraud and sentenced to 15 years' imprisonment, but soon after Zuma became President, Sheik was released from prison in 2009 on medical grounds that he was *terminally ill*, after serving just two years and four months, yet today he remains fit and well and is regularly seen playing golf.

The total value of corruption and theft that has gone on since the ANC took over, I would estimate is at least 1 year's fiscal revenue. Let's limit it to 1 trillion! Some have claimed this could be as much as R3 trillion (around US$200,000,000,000). Imagine what could be achieved to help the poor masses with that sort of money not to mention the knock-on effect it would have had on the economy and resultant increase in GDP.

Chapter 12

Inflation

A topic to which the majority of South Africans turn a blind eye is inflation, just accepting price increases every year on basic items such as water, electricity, petrol and municipal rates and taxes, household and car insurance, and medical insurance, never mind the most basic essential of all namely food. Officially, the most recent inflation figure given by statisticians in SA was just under 5% but on closer inspection, the annual increases in these items over the last few years, a more accurate estimate would be 15%.

According to the January 2021 Household Affordability Index, basic food items such as sugar beans, rice, bread and rice has all seen price hikes from 31% to 68%, way more than the official inflation rate published by Statistics SA. A basic basket of food now costs more than R4,000, exceeding the minimum wage.

The drop in housing prices and the depressed demand for certain goods and services are used by the government to *balance* the inflation figure. This does not reflect the impact on household budgets for essential items, mainly affecting the poor. I long ago mistrusted information given out by any government institutions. I believe SA is in stagflation, namely rising inflation without any economic growth, headed down the same road as Zimbabwe and Venezuela. According to a reliable and honest economist, well-known Magnus Heystek, property values in Sandton have declined by 50% in the last three years, and property prices throughout the country – excluding only the Western Cape – have plummeted by at least one trillion Rand. And yet, your local estate agent will still tell you property prices are rising. Even in the Western Cape, Magnus Heystek says that Cape Town beachfront developers are currently offering reduced prices of R200,000 because of declining sales.

Remainers will argue that the GDP growth for 2021 is headed

toward more than 4.6%, but they seem to totally lose sight of the significant falls in GDP as a result of Covid (apart from ANC corruption and mismanagement), so 4.6% *growth* in GDP is actually no growth at all; it will take about three years just to get back to pre-March 2020 GDP levels.

The state is on the verge of bankruptcy if not already there. Less and less is spent on infrastructure, an essential element for the country to grow. The state housing subsidies are no longer available. After inheriting a sound infrastructure in 1994, there has been practically no maintenance undertaken by the government, with the result that the Railways, for example, is now basically defunct. The lack of new houses for the masses and deteriorating supplies of electricity and water cause almost daily mass protests. Sprawling squatter camps are common. All because the state spends more and more of its budget on public sector wages where productivity is extremely low to non-existent, and on social grants, or dole money for lack of a better description. One top economist's opinion is that if the public sector workforce had the same productivity as in the private sector the economy would grow at 6% annually. One has only to visit the post office and if there is a queue exceeding three people it can take more than half an hour to be served. In the UK that takes 5 minutes. If you need to renew your car licence it's a half-day affair. As for renewing your driver's licence that is an all-day affair, which is the same if you need to visit other government offices like SARS (for income tax) or Home Affairs (for ID and passport matters). The number of wasted man-hours lost to the economy is enormous. The state is not able to collect enough revenue which leads to the burning question from where the money will come. An IMF bailout is required but as alluded to this is unlikely to happen under the ANC government. The answer lies in the money printing machine, which may already be in operation. The state has no option but to pay its employees let alone the social grants, or face an immediate riot.

Every economist will confirm once this happens without any increased productivity the runaway train will just gather speed until it crashes at the end of the line. More and larger notes will have to be printed to keep pace with demand. This even happened in Germany in the late 1920s. As for Zimbabwe, it eventually printed a 40 trillion note which could not buy a loaf of bread. Inflation has featured in the SA economy since 1961; it now takes R9,700 to match the buying power of R100 in 1961.

The ANC now wants to plug the gap by plundering the Public Investment Corporation Fund (PIC) which holds the government pension reserves, to give Eskom a lifeline – what a great *investment* given its track record! At its current value of some R2 trillion, a hundred trillion rand note in the perception would buy out the PIC fifty times. Problem solved. The biggest fear is that after a lifetime of hard work and diligently saving, one's nest egg for retirement can be wiped out in the blink of an eye.

I do not have too much sympathy for the public sector workers whose sheer laziness has severely damaged the economy. Yet the ANC and the President carry on blindly with their socialistic policies. Every member of the party is either a trade unionist, a socialist or a communist and neither knows nor wants to know about basic economics. Every one of them has these socialist visions.

Lebanon is a current example of hyperinflation due to corruption and socialism, with an inflation rate of more than 80%, and the collapse of its currency in 18 months from 1,500 to 60,000 to one versus the US Dollar.

Socialism has never worked and will lead to hyperinflation. Margaret Thatcher once famously said, *The problem with socialism is that you eventually run out of other people's money,* and SA is rapidly running out of money providers.

Chapter 13

RW Johnson's 2015 book

Johnson's book contributed in a big way to my ultimate decision that SA, notwithstanding a happy childhood and many good memories there, was no longer the place I wanted to spend the rest of my days.

The first part of Johnson's book is valuable in the context of building a scenario showing the build-up to where SA is today, but the last four chapters were dynamite and set out with absolute clarity his forecast of the precise situation in which the country now finds itself six years later.

The salient points made by Johnson were the following:

State Repression of Economic Activity

Loading government departments and state-owned enterprises (SOEs) with black employees in the late 1990s led to weak or zero management in the public sector plus a serious drain on the fiscus as salaries escalated exponentially and employment numbers increased to the extent that people did not even know what they were supposed to do. For years the government has bailed out the SOEs with uncountable billions resulting in a huge burden and knock-on effect for the private sector, including massive increases in electricity costs, harbour and airport taxes, hampering trade, productivity and competitiveness. As the state cannot source extra money from the private sector which only has about 1,000 companies and just two million individuals who in reality pay the bulk of the taxes, it must resort to borrowing. The ideology-obsessed ANC has stuck to the ideals of communism which as everyone knows is completely outdated and has failed to embrace

91

capitalism in any form. Most major companies have divested to secure their assets overseas and among these are mining giants BHP Billiton and RTZ. Goldfields gave shares to Zuma's lawyer, other convicted fraudsters, and a convicted bank robber. This diluted the values of all other shares held. SA multinationals all sit on vast profit reserves but are not prepared to reinvest in a country that discourages business.

Meanwhile, in the manufacturing sector, production has halved, with the closure of many major manufacturers – and the resultant loss of jobs – such as Aberdare Cables, Dorbyl Industries, Samancor, Stewarts and Lloyds, Denel which was the leading African arms and military equipment maker, and USCO (which manufactured high-grade steel for gun barrels). In 1994, SA had nuclear capability which is no longer the case; had this continued, SA may have been able today to build its own nuclear power station instead of a quotation of R1 trillion from Russia to do so. Imagine the corruption in such a deal?

In agriculture, SA's farming production has dropped substantially as a result of farm murders, uncertainty on land expropriation issues, and the emigration of farmers. In 1994 there were 60,000 commercial farmers and this number was predicted to drop to 8,000 by 2030. The country's situation is gradually worsening to the point of being unable to feed itself. There are huge tracts of arable land in the Ciskei/Transkei that remain unutilised because the government is not interested.

The View from the IMF

The International Monetary Fund (IMF) is monitoring SA's fiscal management. Out-of-control public service wages must be cut and workers retrenched. The country fares the worst in the world on its expenditure for public service wages as a percentage of GDP. IMF warnings have been ignored. The state has lost control of the police and unions. The SA Democratic Teachers Union (SADTU) upstaged the Minister of Education and brought about the collapse of the public education system. Moody's and major rating agencies have downgraded SA's credit status leading to massive increases in the cost of borrowing which the government is engaged in at an alarming rate. Deteriorating public finances, rising corruption and levels of social and political tensions do not concern the leaders. The current finance minister Tito Mboweni and Cyril Ramaphosa are staunch socialists. The ANC has destroyed the efficient system of the previous government. Without radical reform, the country will find it impossible to fund its fiscal and trading deficits and will not be able to escape its debt trap except through IMF intervention. Former Finance Minister Trevor Manuel in the early-2000s launched his national development plan which found favour with the IMF, but this has been ignored by the ANC government. As lender of last resort to any country, Johnson pointed out SA will never meet the lending criteria of the IMF, including:

- Labour market reform scrapping BEE and affirmative action;
- Immigration laws changed to allow for the massive import of much-needed skills;
- SOEs run profitably or privatised or closed;
- Eskom ensuring a proper supply of electricity;
- Drastic cuts in public sector employment;
- Less red tape for business;
- Reduction of trade union power;
- No land expropriation without compensation;
- No national health insurance scheme couple with health sector reform;
- The eradication of corruption and prosecution from the top to the bottom; and,
- Education system overall.

The BRICS Alternative

If the government thinks it can rely on the so-called Brics Coalition (Brazil Russia India China and SA) to bail it out it is clutching at straws. The country's GDP in 1977 was the 18th highest in the world but by 2013 it had dropped to number 33. China wiped out SA's

93

textile industry. SA cannot compete due to its labour laws and high cost of labour. Russia and China are the two dominant powers, both based on dictatorship models. China has overtaken SA as the world's biggest gold producer. The ANC has always been anti-western. Each country can only have a bailout of double its contribution which in SA's case amounts to a mere R5 billion, with onerous loan conditions attached similar to the IMF's. In effect, SA depends on China, and will only receive a hard bargain. Moreover, China has its own financial woes, with total debt over 240% of GDP, which includes government debt at around 92% of GDP.

Autarchy (Going it Alone)

The country is part of the international system, it is impossible to go the autarchy route; moreover, the parochial narrow-mindedness and socialism are causing the economic collapse.

Zimbabwean Situation

In 1999, when Mugabe had no option than to turn to the IMF, he told it to go to hell rather than accept the loan conditions. Autarchy led to ruin – people starved and fled to other countries. Currency collapse followed hyperinflation with a banknote reaching Zim $400 trillion. SA is different, geographically at the southern tip of Africa with no further migration southwards possible except for the South pole. Secondly, most SAns now live in the major cities and despite ANC talk of expropriating farms, the city dwellers have no idea how to farm or survive as subsistence farmers, unlike some Zimbabweans. South Africans are locked in and the stakes a lot higher than Zimbabwe's.

Scenario accepting IMF bailout

The socialist and communist factions in the ANC would fight an IMF bailout with all their might and if this caused a split in the ANC, the remaining faction would need DA support to govern. Any coalition attempts to abandon detrimental laws, implement radical changes in the public sector and privatise SOEs would lead to huge strikes and violence, especially with the EFF stirring the pot on the left-wing side.

Scenario where ANC majority refuses IMF bailout

Accepting an IMF bailout is in reality an impossibility as this would terminate the ANC's COSATU and Communist Party alliance which comprises two-thirds of the ANC. These two entities would both come to an end. It would also be embarrassing for the ANC to admit it had failed, unlike the apartheid regime.

Going for the Mugabe Option

An IMF bailout would be rejected and ANC members would toe the party line and vote against it for fear of losing their well-paid jobs in parliament. This would ultimately collapse the economy and currency, accompanied by still further unemployment and potentially unprecedented urban unrest. Xenophobic attacks against black foreigners will be far worse involving all areas of the cities. No doubt the ANC would blame the whites and foreign capitalists and probably trigger more expropriation of assets. If companies were nationalised they would soon collapse through lack of management and technical skills. If white billionaires were targeted the ANC would discover most of their money is already offshore.

The ANC definition of liberation is the parasitic elite feathering their nests. Those with wealth are not prepared to share with the needy despite their supposedly left-wing leanings. The only way out of this mess is headlong growth.

Back to the land

As in Zimbabwe, land would be the next target which is already happening. More farmers would leave leading to food scarcity. A hungry man is an angry man. An increasing trade deficit would adversely affect the government's ability to import food and one day in the not-too-distant future, United Nations assistance might be needed.

Loss of Central Control

The state is anaemic and trapped in a downward spiral of low economic growth; the quality of cabinet ministers is extremely low with no coordination in the oversized cabinet. The ANC is unable to deal with large-scale urban unrest due to the ineffective police and army. When hundreds of protests take place, almost daily, they merely stand by and watch and no arrests are ever made despite property damage. An even more effective apartheid security force battled against the masses. History shows it was then and still the case now that no SA government can cope with it. The ANC also does not want to be seen as acting like the old nationalist regime. If the ANC continues with its African nationalism and tries to fix prices and exchange rates, ignoring economic market realities hyperinflation would set in and SA would be back at the IMF's door.

Recognising Reality

Is the ANC prepared to change its ideologies and reform itself by abandoning its stated policies or will it continue on the road to ruin?

Facing the Inevitable

The ANC, with or without the aid of the DA must reform, or it will go further down the Mugabe route. The liberation period has ended and it produced an ANC government quite incapable of proper governance.

Many whites have returned to their contempt for all things African for which one may sympathise given the way they have been treated by the ANC and its policies which it would deny are based on revenge. People express opinions that they regret their previous liberal stance. Johnson points out on the other side of the coin the blacks may lack self-esteem for the way things are (not) working out and be anxious that just maybe the white supremacists were right after all. The following were pinpointed as the cause of the ANC's current stance:

- accepting communist policy as followed by white intellectuals in the 1960s and adopted by the ANC as official policy in 1969;
- a long period of oppression which in turn led to the self-defeating armed struggle, jail for many, and bitterness. The Afrikaners took several generations to get over the Anglo-Boer war and that the same now applies to the blacks.

Changes were inevitable even though they may – no, would – cause considerable hardship. He felt that many Africans are Christians, want law and order, the restoration of the death penalty and liberal democracy in SA.

The above is a summary of points made by Johnson. But was he too optimistic? Time will tell and I sincerely hope Johnson lives to witness the eventual outcome.

Chapter 14

2015 onwards

A lot has happened since Johnson's book. Much of what he predicted came to pass as the country plummeted into an economic and social crisis of unprecedented proportions. He was 100% right that when the stage is reached where the ANC, having destroyed the economy rather than rescuing it, will have to knock on the door of the IMF for a bailout loan to keep the country afloat. As I write this, we know that any such loan will be subject to the necessary reforms being undertaken. The ANC bluntly said in 2020 it will never seek an IMF bailout. This reinforces Johnson's scenario forecast of the ineluctable.

The IMF has repeatedly warned that the ANC cannot keep on borrowing to settle its debts. The last estimate was that debt would reach 65% of GDP by end-2019 which, for SA was considered too high. In the 2021 Budget the new Finance Minister, after he disclosed the deficit had reached nearly 100% and realising the seriousness of the situation, simply laughed his way through his speech, not raising taxes apart from the usual sin taxes (on tobacco and alcohol). He presented a budget showing a deficit of R200 to R300 billion. How this deficit would be covered he did not say; as everyone already knew, only further borrowing could provide (temporary) relief. It seems there is crass ignorance around how compound interest works. The percentage of its budgeted income the government has to spend on interest payments has risen from 13% in 2018 to 21%, second only to the public sector salary bill of 41%. Given the Minister's socialist background, this was hardly surprising. No doubt his hands were firmly tied by the ANC. The State can no longer collect enough tax revenue to cover its obligations and wastefulness. The widening trade deficit compounds the problem. Hardly surprising, seeing all the imported fancy vehicles of the elite while the country's exports are dropping off the cliff. The only industry still worth its salt is motor manufacturing; the government has learnt not to interfere too much because the motor companies will simply pack up and leave, as has happened in a few instances.

Given the depreciating rand, it is becoming more and more difficult to pay for imports, particularly as less foreign exchange comes into the country. In 2015 Eskom's debt was R200 billion. This ballooned to R480 billion by the end of 2020, including its annual operating loss of at least R25 billion and cumulative debt interest. An example of the scale of corruption is the son of a friend of my wife who was contracted as an IT expert by Eskom; when he arrived there, he was booked into an exclusive and exorbitant boutique hotel – owned by one of the directors of Eskom, cashing in. He also observed the total inactivity of all staff working at Eskom, even the sweepers leaning idly on their brooms. Since 2007, load shedding, not having enough electricity supply, has come back to haunt the country. The two new power stations, Medupi and Kaliso, have been poorly constructed and will not produce the output originally planned; the budget ballooned from R162 billion to R450 billion and these stations are still not fit for purpose. Koeberg, the nuclear power station near Cape Town, is now past its *sell-by* date and its future hangs by a thread; standard safety precautions and essential maintenance are being ignored. Chernobyl and Fukushima loom. The taxpaying population is seriously fed up with the situation, but there's nothing they can do about this – other than for those who can afford to become self-sufficient. A friend recently spent R650,000 on solar panels and powerful batteries so he is now completely off the grid. Eskom has admitted it will take three years to sort out its electricity supply problems, but experts reckon on at least 5 years. The bottom line is it is not going to be resolved until they get rid of half the workforce, reduce the outrageous salaries, increase productivity and enforce payment by black township dwellers. This cannot be achieved without the required skilled workers already chased away by the ANC. Only then will they be able to ensure a decent supply of power to move the country forward. The most disturbing feature of this mismanagement and the corruption *a la* the Guptas is that it has contributed greatly to the recession in which the country now finds itself. Before Covid arrived in March 2020, the previous two quarters of consecutive contraction in the economy officially constituted a recession. Eskom's operational loss was a major contributor. The government declares it is going to re-industrialise SA to kickstart the economy but, of course, without first sorting out the electricity supply, they will put the cart before the horse.

Theft of Electrical Power is Rife – Acknowledgments to researchgate.net

When one looks at some of the other countries in Africa such as Kenya, reportedly growing at 6% annually, the ANC should hang its head in shame. But that is another story.

The last of the big credit ratings agencies, namely Moody's, has officially downgraded SA's international credit risk to junk status. This resulted in a huge outflow of investment funds because international institutions such as pension schemes are not allowed to invest in a country with junk status. Predictions were that there would be an outflow of at least $10 billion or about 150 billion Rs. Apart from this loss, the country will be quite unable to attract new funds. By all accounts, it will take at least 5 years of rectification before the rating can be upgraded. And junk status is not the lowest rating. What is the picture going to look like in the foreseeable future?

For many years SA's interest rates have been substantially higher than most countries, resulting in it being an attractive investment destination (provided the necessary currency hedges were in place). With the downgrade and the reduction of interest rates to try and ignite the economy, I do not see investors falling over themselves to pour money into the country. Soon after Ramaphosa became President he announced he had received overseas pledges of R100 billion in investments to expand the economy. I wonder why nothing has happened since?

Talking about the new President one has to look at what happened in the 2019 general election to try and make an assessment. Because Ramaphosa occupied the number one position in the party it was a foregone conclusion he would continue as president.

When the ANC won the election with 57% of the vote it was time for Ramaphosa to announce his new cabinet. He got rid of a couple of the ministers who were seen as dead wood but promptly added another four Deputy Ministers who have proved no better, notwithstanding the stated intention of reducing costs which never happened. The most disturbing thing about the whole setup in the ANC National Executive Committee (NEC) comprising the top 6 who make all major decisions, is that at least four of the top 6, including Mabuza, Magashule, Mantashe and Jessie Durante are all unprosecuted criminals of the highest order and Jacob Zuma's allies. Ramaphosa probably had to appoint David Mabuza as his Vice President to appease the Communist Party and trade union behemoth COSATU.

101

In recent times Johann Rupert made a statement about disinvesting from the country for fear of a Mabuza presidency, but then again with his companies' listings on overseas stock exchanges, he cannot be overly concerned.

There is talk it is only a matter of time before Ramaphosa is ousted like Mbeki and Zuma were. For the last 2 years, Ramaphosa has made all these flowery speeches promising much but delivering nothing. He keeps talking about reforms and providing jobs but with COSATU and the Communist Party firmly in control of the ANC, he knows that as much as he might want (if indeed he does) there is precious little he can do. The question remains does he really care for the poor or is he only in it for power and greed?

A lot of people voted for the ANC because of the promise of a new dawn but to quote Johnson, *South Africa can either choose to have an ANC government or it can have a modern industrial economy. It cannot have both.* I just find it amazing that anyone with common sense still votes for a party with a shambolic record of destruction and misgovernance. And they call it democracy!

The other noteworthy outcome of the 2019 election was the lack of support for the one party that might have been able to do something positive, namely the DA, which dropped from approximately 21% to 17% of the vote. This was very surprising given its track record of running the Western Cape so well. Many whites voted for the right-wing Freedom Front Party, quite meaningless given the small size of the party. The biggest concern as we have seen was the increase of the EFF from 6% to nearly 12%.

In the next general election, it will probably be the main opposition party, except in the remote event Ramaphosa is sincere in his concern for the plight of the poor and does the right thing by pushing ahead with reforms, leading to a split in the ANC. This would leave it without a power base and the depleted ANC's only option would be to team up with the DA to lead the people to the promised land (of 1994). No doubt the remnants of the ANC would link up with the EFF and the outcome of an election if this materialised would indeed be interesting. SA might then even have true democracy. If this does not happen only the Zimbabwe route beckons.

Reportedly, in the last 2 years, two thousand SA individuals with a net worth of between R10 and R100 million have left the country which tells us many people are not hanging around to see what happens. Every individual who leaves SA means, on average, a loss of R1.2 million to the fiscus – not to mention Value Added Tax, their expenditure on fuel and accompanying levies, their employment (very often) of other people terminated, and other economic activities. In today's world, people are mobile and not location-dependent. The non-ANC aligned blacks and whites are leaving for pastures greener simply to escape the draconian labour laws (which make it well-nigh impossible to get rid of any employee and the high minimum wages), the affirmative action laws which prevent those leaving from obtaining employment irrespective of their qualifications, rampant crime levels, and to live where they will no longer be attacked based on their race or political alignment.

The outflow of funds has become a torrent and I would not be surprised if harsher foreign exchange controls are introduced which will be disastrous for the economy and the exchange rate. After the recent news regarding the Land Expropriation Act and the NHI scheme, the number of people leaving has gathered momentum. One major firm that specialises in UK immigration has been flooded with applications from South Africans.

The government does not even know how many people have left as they just quietly slip out of the country on a one-way ticket. When my wife booked our tickets we were surprised to learn the travel agent we normally dealt with had just left for Australia. I also then learnt my auditor was making plans to head for New Zealand. Both are Afrikaners so the exodus is not limited to people with dual nationality.

In 2017, a wealthy Indian family, the Guptas, was exposed after plundering the country with the full support of Zuma and his cronies. They fled the country never to be seen again. In typical fashion, the government has now set up the Zondo commission. As has been pointed out, the money has gone and when its findings are known it is doubtful whether any of the top dogs will be prosecuted, more specifically Zuma, currently the hot topic of contempt proceedings for failure to appear before Judge Zondo. What is certain is that any recovery of money will be negligible or nil. Sanjeev Gupta has again hit the news in 2021 with a loss faced by Greensill Capital the supply chain finance specialist now teetering on the brink of collapse, with *no value* against capital finance of €2 Billion advanced to Gupta's company.

The agricultural sector and the country's food supply are threatened. Ongoing farm attacks carry on unabated and the government seems powerless to do anything about it while remaining in denial of any problem, it being a common belief that these attacks are part of an orchestrated land grab agenda. Certainly, the slogan *Kill the Boer, kill the Farmer* is not deemed hate speech by the government and people do not get punished for its use – even while the masses are taking this literally. It was recently reported these attacks only take place on remote smallholdings and not on commercial farms, but when Agriculture SA and institutions like Afriforum express concern about the attacks, which are at best only superficially investigated by the police and seldom reported in the media, one begins to realise how serious is the situation. I was shocked recently to learn of the murder of Charles Hart, a farmer all his life from the Cathcart area. Charles and I were in the same hostel at Dale College in the 1960s. A disturbing feature of all this is the ever-dwindling skills loss, let alone the drop in food production and a corresponding rise in food prices.

Due to my wife's disability, I always used to do our shopping in SA and noted a steep hike in the supermarket prices especially around 2016 when, for example, the bacon price shot up from R12 to over R20 and then R30. Food inflation is currently 17%. During our stay in the UK over the past year, I have not noticed any price increases whatsoever.

When it comes to the SOEs the ANC is determined to carry on regardless, pouring money down the drain while consistently refusing to reform. Economics will sort them all out eventually. On 5 December 2019, the government announced SAA was placed under bankruptcy protection; the airline did not turn a profit from 2011 and finally ran out of money, despite annual bailouts by the government and having the monopoly on various routes. The losses in the last few years were over R20 billion yet the government tries to hold on by appointing new CEOs and boards of directors who come up with meaningless plans before leaving and being awarded huge payouts. I was astounded to learn one of these CEOs started as a cabin stewardess a short time before her elevation to the top position in the company.

As predicted, in the local elections, the ANC lost its control in cities like PE, Johannesburg and Pretoria. Unfortunately, the DA has not been able to gain outright majorities leading to coalition governance which the ANC aided by the EFF invariably manages to collapse within a short while. The result has been very poor performances at the local government level. If the government cannot run these cities it stands no chance of running the country as a whole. As some sage commented, the ANC cannot run a bath, never mind a city.

Chapter 15

Synopsis - My Conclusions

Having now reached the crossroads, does the country make an about-turn or does it continue headlong into an economic crisis with many years of pain and strife to follow.

In trying to assess the road ahead one must consider the following:

The ANC Government as It Now Exists

ANC policies since the middle of the last century have remained unchanged, in adhering to extreme left-wing communism, socialism and trade unionism. In 1969 the ANC adopted communism as its official policy. In 1992 the 69% of whites who voted in favour of political change to include the majority did not know or realise the new Constitution would not safeguard their rights against future communist policies. History has proven that communism, socialism and trade unionism do not work and even the biggest geographical block, the USSR collapsed due to the economics involved. We also know that every high-ranking ANC member is a fanatical left-winger neither seeking nor prepared to change.

In 1994 when the ANC took over, I did not mind who ruled the country provided they did so properly to ensure peace, harmony and prosperity for all. No one then realised the ANC would continue on its pre-chosen path and consequently destroy the economy.

When the former nationalist government was fighting its border wars, the *communist threat* was always used as a danger and indeed, the rationale behind fighting the border wars. I doubt the National Party envisaged the communists as represented by the ANC but rather the Cubans and the Russians, or they would certainly not have given up power so easily if they had a crystal ball. Sadly, history shows us that they had a point.

A few years ago, I remarked to a retired bank manager that as long as the ANC continued on its present path in running the country SA was doomed.

Apart from the *ineptocracy*, corruption is now so widespread and entrenched, with everyone from top to bottom involved and at the stage where the government is powerless to *stop the gravy train* even if it wants to. Many grandiose speeches delivered, but no action. SA stands *sans égal* as the most corrupt country in the world.

In the early days of ANC rule, nearly everyone said it was okay for the ANC to be corrupt as the Nationalist politicians had also filled their boots. History now shows they were in a far lower league compared to the ANC. The old ANC stalwart Oliver Tambo expressed that he was more worried about a corrupt ANC government than anything else.

The Even Greater Racial Divide

Given SA's history of how its population is made up of nomadic tribes from the North clashing with the white settlers, there was always going to be a clash of interests.

However, the forty-odd years of apartheid seem to be the defining years of SA's history, fuelling untold hatred among its inhabitants. We all know apartheid was morally and defensively wrong. Many whites voted against and were against it. What has transpired since the ANC took over is no less a terrible shame and history will show it missed a huge opportunity to make SA one of the top nations in the world. Instead, the ANC has reduced the country to the bottom rung of the ladder, in what many might describe as revenge tactics against the whites. I do not think it initially set out on this route, especially during Nelson Mandela's time at the helm, but as time has gone by its antiquated socialist policies have led to the ANC blaming the whites increasingly for everything that has gone wrong.

The Truth and Reconciliation Commission, while acclaimed internationally as a success, among many blacks it also stoked future racism by constant reference to *You see what you did to us*. The intention was to address the past, achieve reconciliation, then move on. Instead, it seems to have become a blueprint for playing the eternal victim card. The country needed to let bygones be bygones and for the ANC to get on with proper governance.

In the first few years of ANC rule, I think all South Africans were prepared to embrace each other for the common good. The 1995 Rugby World Cup at Ellis Park was probably the highest point of non-racism the country achieved. Since then racism has steadily become more entrenched. The 2019 euphoria of winning its third World Cup evaporated so quickly that it was back to real life for most people the very next day, again worrying about where their next crust of bread would come from.

In 1986, at the height of apartheid, the PE Golf Club declared itself open to membership by all races and in the late-1980s, a black member Precious Makwabe won the Club Singles Championship. He was a fine golfer and a perfect gentleman, against whom I played in the Championship one year, losing to him in the semi-final. Sadly, he was one of the few blacks who took up the club's offer and became a member, and sadder still was that he died in a car accident not long after he became Club Champion. Even today, there is only a small number of black golfers in SA.

As the years have gone by not only did ANC policies impoverish the whole population but they also led to mass unemployment amongst its supporters.

This in turn fuelled racism on both sides of the divide, each blaming the other for their predicaments. The ANC has contributed in no uncertain terms by openly blaming everything on apartheid and the whites. At election times this has become even more intense – and led to the rise of Julius Malema's EFF. The ANC grossly underestimated him when they expelled Malema from their Party. Since then the anti-white rhetoric that has spewed out of his mouth has been unbelievable. His sheer hate speech goes unpunished, including *Kill the Boer, Kill the Farmer* publicised across the world.

The government passed a law that anyone who engaged in hate speech against another racial group would be guilty of a crime. In practice, this law sadly only applies to the whites, I am sad to say, the sole demographic convicted of any hate crimes. Evidence of this is the way an estate agent Penny Mellon and another SA of Greek origin were severely sanctioned by the courts with ridiculous fines of over R100,000 which they could not afford to pay, in the case of the Greek man for using the *K-word* thousands of miles from SA in a tweet on Twitter.

All this adds to growing distrust and tension between the races.

About 2 years ago at a golfing tournament, I heard some of the worst hate speech used by a white Afrikaner in a small rural town. He was upset by the fact there was no water at home as the supply had been cut off for the umpteenth time due to the inefficiencies of the local ANC municipality. What he said (translated from Afrikaans) was that *These useless f------g k------s should be happy that we call them k------s!*

Malema has now coined the phrase *white monopoly capital* which is nonsensical in its intended meaning that the whites have all the money and the blacks have nothing. His latest buzz phrase is Radical Economic Transformation (RET). There are now numerous black millionaires in the country. And most of them have achieved this status as we have seen without having to work for it. Malema is one of the upper classes living a life of luxury – despite he and other EFF members (for the sake of appearance) donning red worker overalls when appearing in Parliament.

In the 1990s I drove into the black townships to see clients and was never concerned for my safety. The way things have developed, and

I blame the ANC for the heightened tension, I would no longer dare venture into these areas unaccompanied by a black friend. It is back to the dark old days it seems. Racism is not only limited to black on white but the Indians and the Coloureds have also been given a raw deal, left behind the blacks in the entitlement queue.

My biggest fear is that racism is now so ingrained in the majority – black and white, it is going to be impossible to reverse this until a new political dispensation is in place.

Democracy Gone Wrong

In 1994 everyone, indeed the whole world hailed the birth of democracy in SA. Whether one likes it or not, universal suffrage was never going to work in SA under ANC rule, despite the *non-racial society* espoused in its Freedom Charter. The masses have become even less educated with the collapse of the education system; one cannot help but wonder if there is an agenda to dumb down the population. Votes based on merit (as put forward by the Merit Party) could never be accepted by the ANC. Let us not forget that the ANC was a liberation movement and except for Nelson Mandela and a few others, it was simply not equipped to run the country. Yet they knew what to do when it came (and comes) to plundering the economy! Before the 1994 election, they openly said they were the only government in waiting and this should have been a power hunger warning sign. The world wanted change and got it through economic sanctions, not through the liberation movement although it played a part. I fear world leaders will have more to sort out in SA in the years to come.

When it comes to election time the ANC, and also the EFF, draw up lists of their cadres – people favoured through their connections to the party hierarchy and therefore appointed members of parliament without the necessary skills or ability. They know how to spend their fat salaries and allowances on luxury motor cars and the like. Of course, they only get the position if they toe the party line which means voting in favour of whatever is tabled before parliament by the party – that is if they are present to vote, absenteeism being the rule. They never dare question whether it is good or bad for the country. In Zuma's time, there was a female parliamentarian supposedly made an MP because she had done him a favour; she never uttered a word throughout her tenure in parliament and today enjoys a healthy retirement pension.

When the pressure was building up on Zuma to quit, a no-confidence motion brought by the DA had to be voted on to try and force him out. Despite all his wrongdoings the ANC as a matter of principle still voted against the motion. However, about 10 or so ANC members had some conscience and voted for the motion in a secret ballot. The hierarchy announced it would find out who these transgressors were and punish them. The outcome has never been revealed.

The ANC simply bulldozes whatever legislation it wants through parliament. The only time it gets any real opposition is when at the start of proceedings the EFF rises on a point of order on some obscure subject which the Speaker is unable or given the chance to answer for being drowned out by the noise. It then descends into chaos and often leads to parliamentary security being called in to eject the EFF. There has been physical abuse at times. The EFF and even the DA have on occasion staged walkouts. The joke is that ANC and EFF members address each other as *Honourable Member* when in reality it would be difficult to find a single honourable person among them.

Talking about the Speaker, I mentioned how dishonourable was the previous one who fraudulently acquired her fake driving licence. This position is always filled by the appointment of a staunch and senior ANC member, unlike in proper democracies such as in the UK where all members vote and it sometimes happens that a member of the opposition gets the nod and still acts impartially.

We have seen the results of the last general election with the ANC retaining 57% of the popular vote. This was achieved although anywhere else in the world they would have been thrown out. The

111

drop in the number of votes is attributed to the masses rather abstaining than vote for another party such as the DA. The latter appears to be in decline, labelled a *white party* and a vote for the DA would be seen as giving up their hard-won *freedom*. Sadly, they now have less freedom than ever. More people would rather have food in their stomachs than a vote. They do not grasp the situation. The leadership of the DA has gone backwards since the days of Van Zyl Slabbert and Tony Leon (who has written a book which includes the statistic that bad governments on average last no more than 30 years, and he predicts that in 2024, the ANC will lose the general election). The disturbing aspect is that even when it had a black leader, Mmusi Maimane, who seemed a very plausible leader, the masses did not vote for him. The DA axed Maimane after the disastrous last general election, blaming him for its poor performance. And now it has a white leader John Steenhuisen once more which only entrenches the racial divide.

We have witnessed the upsurge of the EFF and as things deteriorate with steadily increasing unemployment its political base can only grow. ANC policies have become more aligned with those of the EFF and a reverse takeover of the ANC is on the cards. The ANC would first have to lose its overall majority – hard to imagine given that free and fair elections are a thing of the past with missing ballot boxes found opened and strewn around the place. Democracy only works when the loser is prepared to give up power, follow the rule of law, and the judiciary will (or can) enforce this if necessary.

The Centre for Risk Analysis headed by Dr Frans Cronje, who advises their clients on the risks of investing in SA, thinks the ANC could *lose* the next election in 2024, or at the latest in 2029, but as I have set out above, the ANC will not relinquish power anytime soon. On the contrary, as with Zanu PF in Zimbabwe, it intends to hold onto power, even if this needs the help of the army and police.

All of this shows the democracy envisaged has not happened and SA will continue to be ruled badly for years to come.

The ANC's Economic Disaster and the IMF

The ANC's disastrous policies have effectively bankrupted the country and all SOEs. It will not accept IMF loan conditions. Ramaphosa has often spoken about reforms none of which goes to the heart of the problems. The likely scenario is quantitative easing, namely printing more money. Unlike the UK and USA, SA is unable to support quantitative easing through increased economic activity and productivity.

The ANC recently announced officially it will not entertain any IMF bailout. The simple reason is that those in control of the country, the Ace Magashules and David Mabuzas plus all the communists and trade unionists would never allow this as it would mean the end of the Communist Party and the power of the trade unions. Where does that leave the President? Three years ago, there were high hopes he would split the ANC and if he then did not have enough backing, he would join hands with rational thinking people perhaps including the DA. It appears he does not have the gumption to even attempt such a move. The record shows Ramaphosa stood idly by as Vice President while Zuma ransacked the state's coffers. Already under his watch, he has introduced the minimum wage and land expropriation bills, further taking the country down the road to economic disaster. One can only, therefore, assume he is a staunch socialist or just in it for what he can get out of it.

The lone conclusion is the ANC will increasingly have to find more money as politically it cannot afford any default in payment of public service salaries and the social grants; the only solution will be the *Mugabe printing machine* with disastrous consequences.

The Demise of the Minority Groups in South Africa

It would not be amiss to say a word or two about the ANC's agenda on minority groups that formed the majority of the former middle classes. As we have seen, huge numbers of people, at least I million whites alone, have been driven into poverty and squatter camps.

According to some people, like Scott Balson of The Loving LifeTV channel, it is an ongoing gradual process of genocide, particularly against the whites but also the coloured and Indian groups.

One only has to analyse the ridiculous regulations regarding the Covid pandemic, such as a total ban on alcohol (impossible to police as against the masses), and the 9 pm curfew (again, simply ignored by blacks living cheek by jowl), to realise that it is 'one rule for thee and one rule for me.' The taxi owners and township dwellers can do as they please but in a bizarre reverse racism, people of other colour groups are having their businesses destroyed, being locked down/up both in their homes and for the slightest transgression of Covid restrictions.

Suffice it to say the ANC has almost succeeded to the point where there is hardly any fight back from minority groups or even big business.

Even the DA in parliament as the official opposition has become toothless. When Covid eventually passes the ANC will have succeeded in destroying many thousands of businesses and have the nation exactly way it wants it, akin to what Mugabe did in Zimbabwe – especially after all the new laws are passed, including amending the constitution, the implementation of the national health scheme, the expropriation of assets and nationalisation of the Reserve Bank. As we know, 60% of the whites are the Afrikaners and unless I stand, hopefully, corrected in due course, they seem to have no fight left in them, not that I advocate a call to violence. They seem to lack the will to resist the changes taking place. The stage will shortly be reached where the ANC will control all aspects of everyone's life and no individual freedoms will be left.

The problem is that the Afrikaners are geographically widespread and there does not appear to be any unity. One notable exception might be the band of *Suidlanders* in the Cape and the *Boere Legion* but it is debatable what they can achieve politically, if anything, apart from defending their properties.

So, in essence, it begs the question what does it mean to be a South African today?

I would answer as follows:

- Living in a country where the rainbow nation and unity disappeared a long time ago;
- Living in a socialist/communist dictatorship where poverty prevails among the masses;
- Living in fear, both of personal safety and loss of property;
- Where your rights and freedoms have been taken away;
- Where your democratic vote has become meaningless;
- Contributing taxes to the fiscus, knowing most of this will either be lost to corruption or spent on the ANC cadres and welfare benefits for the masses; and,
- Where national pride has been eroded and where it is difficult to support national sporting teams which are not chosen on merit.

The Final Countdown

The clock ticking since 1994 is getting louder and faster. As in (i) to (iv) of this chapter, there is no turning back for the ANC. People living in the country day-to-day do not notice the small changes that take place all the time. Ramaphosa has become famous for the pre-CODESA article he wrote about the boiled frog approach so that whites, coloureds and Asians will not even be aware of the changes slowly but surely engulfing them. The problem is that most people in SA and I refer especially to *the remainers*, live in a bubble. While they acknowledge things are going from bad to worse, they are the fortunate ones with the financial means (for now) to cling to their lifestyles, live in a spacious home with servants, afford expensive security protection measures, shop in modern malls, visit elite restaurants and select sports clubs. They perceive they are not threatened by violent crime. There is still a great degree of polarisation between those who stay and those who leave.

Meanwhile, the number of no-go areas increases, including the beachfront of my old town PE.

As the whites become poorer their squatter camps grow. A friend of mine spends most of his week providing food and shelter at an old disused caravan park, for the whites and coloureds who have fallen on hard times, mainly for the reason that the government discriminates against whites and coloureds when it comes to food and other aid relief. One sees more and more white people begging at the traffic lights.

The law of the jungle is fast becoming a reality. Khayelitsha, a huge squatter camp in Cape Town, is an absolute eyesore and a shock for foreign visitors travelling on the N1; it is ruled by the gangs and the authorities have lost control. I witnessed that it is often impossible to evict people even with a court order. The street committees decide who will reside in a particular home. Who will dare move into a house with a death threat hanging over them? How long can some semblance of order be maintained? Certainly, looking to the courts is not going to help much if at all.

There will be no intervention from the outside world and events will be left to simply unfold. Countries have a policy of not interfering in the internal affairs of others – except when it suits them.

The only hope is a regime change at some point. However, I think the ANC will rule for many years to come by entrenching a one-party state and dictatorship.

Even the Roman Empire fell. Eventually. The ANC's increasing persecution of the white means any reconstruction process will take that much longer. Meanwhile, SA plunges into another Zimbabwe/ Venezuela situation, where people fled huge social unrest. This is all thanks to socialism, and not embracing the whites in 1994 or acknowledging the role they had to play in taking the country forward. Helen Zille was correct when she said there are positives to be taken from colonisation. The original white settlers were responsible for building the country from scratch into a modern developed country, only to have the ANC break it down. As my senior advocate friend remarked, when the white settlers arrived in 1652 the indigenous peoples had never yet seen a wheel. The sole difference between whites and blacks is cultural. Nothing else. If not for the settlers the modern towns and cities along the south coast would only consist of the mud huts still seen today on the coastal hills of Transkei.

Lord Acton's saying, *Power tends to corrupt, and absolute power corrupts absolutely* in 1887 has never been more relevant than today when discussing the ANC. Its corruption and economic policies are proof of this saying. On the economic front, no one has taken into account that nearly 30 years down the line many young, educated and skilled people have emigrated, lost to the country with no job opportunities for them. At the top end of the scale, people are retiring so, in just a few short years, this huge vacuum has been created leaving insufficient skills to run the country.

The great pity about SA with its natural resources is that given the way the country was in 1994, it should have one of the top economies in the world. In contrast, China has shown what can be achieved in 30 years with an open market policy embracing capitalism.

The capital of the Philippines, Manila, is slowly eradicating its slums and providing huge employment opportunities for its population. Singapore is just an island and look at what has happened there. It is one of the most progressive cities in the world. As for India, it has grown economically, with 300 million of its vast population taken out of poverty. Indeed, if SA had followed suit, today it would not have slums like Khayelitsha in Cape town or Alexandra in Johannesburg.

It is never too late to have an about-turn. Already Vietnam and Mexico are seen as the next economic hotspots in the world having hungry and cheap labour forces taking over former Chinese production due to China's escalating labour costs.

My greatest hope was that the ANC would see the folly of its ways but it has become clear there will be many years of hardship and bloodshed ahead, following in the footsteps of its northern neighbours.

The real miracle will be when the ANC's rule comes to an end and then it will take many years to rehabilitate the country and, hopefully, catch up with the rest of the world.

Chapter 16

COVID-19

Since reaching my conclusions above, the world was devastated by the Covid-19 virus which started in China. Without discussing the rights and wrongs of the way various governments around the world have dealt with the pandemic and here I include SA, let it be said that the imminent economic collapse of the country has been accelerated as a result. SA does not have the necessary financial muscle to help its citizens as in the USA, UK, and Europe where people and businesses have been propped up with government loans and grants during the lockdowns. At the outset of the pandemic, President Ramaphosa announced a R500 billion package to bolster the economy. Quite where he was going to get the money from remains a mystery. When this was announced, it was mentioned that some departments would have to receive less than their original budgets. It follows that this means less infrastructure spend and in turn less economic development. The balance was to come from more borrowing, pushing the debt to GDP ratio towards 100%. The country received a US$4.3 billion loan from the IMF repayable in 5 years but as Covid relief, without strings attached. However, as everyone knows, this money was dished out to all the ANC cadres to supply medical equipment to hospitals at exorbitant prices. Cadres with no experience in the medical field quickly formed companies to supply goods and services at 10 x market value. Corruption continues unabated even in times of crisis and need. And as many will testify, whites were specifically excluded from any Covid-related aid. The police were used to prevent even private food aid from reaching white squatter camps.

The effect of the lockdowns as a result of the virus will be felt for years to come. Estimates include a drop of 10% in 2020/2021 GDP, and that it will take about 5 years just to get back to where the country was at the start of the pandemic. Figures from Statistics SA can no longer be believed. Knowledgeable economists report the real unemployment rate has risen from 40% to 50%. Income tax collections have dropped alarmingly with fewer people paying tax and numerous businesses closing. Increased government spending carries on at an alarming rate. The budget at the beginning of the year allowed for a R1.2 trillion tax collection and a spend of R1.4 trillion, creating another massive deficit. By all accounts, R1.8 trillion has been spent and the fiscus will be lucky to collect more than R1 trillion; at a time when the national debt is approaching R5 trillion. The finance minister produced two meaningless interim budgets promising not to increase public sector wages but not giving any detail as to how he will balance the books; 29,000 public service employees currently each earn R1 million or more annually. The trade unions on which the ANC relies for its powerbase are at its throat. No prizes on guessing who will win this battle. The pandemic has resulted in most people now far worse off – apart from the ANC comrades on full pay and their looting of the soft loan from the IMF for Covid-relief. Many would argue the lockdowns were mainly aimed at further financially destroying the remaining middle-class. Certainly, the way the lockdown regulations were enforced bears testimony to this. A major police operation, including a helicopter, to arrest a solitary (white) surfer, after stepping on a beach was declared *unlawful* – while black taxi operators remained legally free to carry up to 16 people in one vehicle at the same time. The original Covid regulation stipulated a maximum of 7 taxi passengers but the Taxi Association ignored this with contempt, and the police were allegedly powerless to enforce compliance. Zuma's ex-wife Nkosazana Dlamini-Zuma led the world as Minister of Cooperative Governance and Traditional Affairs in totally banning alcohol and cigarette sales supposedly to fight the coronavirus, which only fuelled the black market to provide these at inflated prices. Many rumours circulated that Ms Zuma, a SA billionaire, had a finger in the illicit sales pie, which included her son named Edward from her former marriage to Jacob Zuma.

Some recent *lowlights* in South Africa include:

In April 2020 alone, 400 schools were vandalised and burnt down, with hundreds more schools destroyed by protesters before and since. Rebuilding these schools is not in the budget.

A survey revealed only one per cent of pupils in their 4th year of learning are at the international average level in science and maths, two crucial subjects for the future development of the country.

The latest final year school results reflect around 70% of school learners who passed their final exams, but the dropout rate is so high the real pass rate is only 44% of the learners who began school 12 years before.

The pandemic resulted in the total failure of the public health system. Hospitals were overwhelmed, people died in hospital corridors and many died at home for lack of nursing staff and PPE, despite there being a surplus of beds thanks to the likes of Volkswagen building a field hospital with 3,300 beds. These beds were never used.

At the same time as the police were enforcing lockdown restrictions in the white and coloured suburbs, in the black townships, the crowds were holding coronavirus parties in the streets with a conspicuous lack of police visibility.

The official number of Covid-related deaths was 51,000. The CEO of Discovery Health stated this figure was at least double, taking into account the number of excess deaths in the country over the preceding year.

My former secretary has serious heart problems. Three scheduled operations at a public hospital were postponed at the last minute. Covid is the excuse, and I hope she lives to survive the pandemic and finally undergo her heart surgery.

Crime and violence continue unabated. In SA, crime does pay

handsomely for most criminals. Despite the lockdowns, serious crime, including farm murders, increased by about 7% according to the police minister.

A standoff between the EFF and the farming community in the town of Senekal took place recently after a young white farmer was brutally murdered and his body hung on a telephone pole. The police were out in force to prevent a clash between the opposing parties. Julius Malema continued stirring things up (with the implicit blessing of the ANC) and the EFF transferred its attention to a multi-racial school in Brackenfell in the Cape for allegedly being racist by holding a dance not attended by any black pupils despite their being invited. The hate speech and antics of the EFF continue unpunished and the racial divide increases.

In 2020, 23,000 long-term prisoners were released on early parole irrespective of whether or not they were rehabilitated, on the grounds of insufficient accommodation to house them. This can only fuel an increase in crime.

An amazing statistic is there are now over 100,000 security companies operating in the country, turning over R2.5 billion annually.

Another phenomenon is the ever-increasing number of young black children begging at traffic lights. In many cases, this is due to child trafficking and these poor children hand over a certain minimum amount each day, with any balance retained on which to survive. The gangs behind this rake in millions. Liberal whites think they are supporting the poor.

When the ongoing Zondo Commission questioned Dudu Myeni, the former SA Airways boss about her involvement with Zuma, her answers were nonsensical. When asked what she did at work, she said she mainly read the newspapers and various books; she was then asked how much she got paid to read the newspapers and she replied her salary was a matter of public record at 2.5 million Rs a year.

The whole commission is farcical, cost to date almost R800 million.

ANC councillor Andile Lungisa was recently freed from prison after serving two months of a 2-year sentence for serious assault.

In November 2020, a municipal by-election for some 20 seats resulted in gains for the ANC.

The government continues to pass laws it cannot police or administer.

Four important Acts soon to be law are: 1. The Electoral Procedure Act to allow for digital elections, so the whole electoral system will be open to easy manipulation and entrench the ANC remaining in power; 2. The Prescribed Assets Act to force pension funds to *invest* in government funding, including propping up the SOEs and pay for its much-touted infrastructure spend to kickstart the economy; 3. The Reserve Bank Act introduced by Julius Malema to allow for its nationalisation; and, 4. The Expropriation of Land Act already well on its way. It will be interesting to see how the ANC implements this in practice. We know that if it follows the Zimbabwean route of land grabs the economy will collapse in no time at all. One has also to consider commercial banks are owed trillions by property owners.

Bridgestone Tyre Company (formerly Firestone) in 2020 announced its closure in PE with another 400 jobs lost. Deloitte's has also closed, citing insufficient work.

In 1994, SA was the 13th largest economy in the world; it dropped to 33rd in 2015 and is now the 44th. Under the heading of international competitiveness, SA has dropped from 60 to 141. Unsurprising that no one wants to do business with the country apart from needing its minerals.

Only 3.5% of the population of at least 65 million pays tax and of this figure 3% pay 97% of income tax, hardly a recipe for entrenching socialism.

123

Only 4% of the people in the predominantly black area of Alexandria in Johannesburg pay their electricity bills.

As far as SA Airways is concerned the ANC had to throw in the towel although not completely. After propping up this SOE to the tune of over R50 billion the government has undertaken to pay its administrators an amount of R10.5 billion to settle SAA's debts including retrenchment packages for thousands of workers, in return for which SAA has secured a small fleet about 20% of its original size under a new name. How it will make a profit is anyone's guess. Meanwhile, the government has been stalling on making this payment.

Almost everyone stopped paying their TV licences and the SA Broadcasting Corporation (SABC) faced bankruptcy. The government wants to add R50 per month to every household utility bill on the assumption that everyone watches TV. Most people pay their municipal accounts to avoid having their electrical and water services terminated. In the black townships, there are *spiderwebs* of electrical wiring to supply free electricity to most homes and businesses there.

The ANC has passed its BBEEE law whereby if a company wants to do business with the government it must be at least 51% black-owned. Companies are additionally to be forced to employ a minimum number of black people based on their demographic representation in the area. The former DA leader, Mmusi Maimane was outspokenly anti-BBEEE, but the latest revelation is that he has just been made a 51% stakeholder in a substantial BBEEE company…

Big business and the major banks are in collusion with the government to effect all this and feather their own nests, including ANC members as directors on the boards of these corporations. One of Nedbank's directors was, in 1997, an advisor to the government and strongly promoted BEE policies; his reward, a directorship in one of the Big Five banks.

The mayor of Durban was recently implicated in a R400 million corruption scandal but, typically, the ANC responded that she is not guilty until so proven. Meanwhile, the ANC has given her a prominent position in the provincial legislature.

In 2021, the National Lottery rolled over to about R113 million and lo and behold the winning numbers were 5678910 with no less than 20 winners each receiving R5.7 million. This incredible *coincidence* was to be investigated by the Gambling Commission but nothing further has been heard. It has been shown that the lottery awards made in recent years to supposedly needy beneficiaries were all to the advantage of ANC cadres.

The Road Accident Fund has been plundered. There was a law firm De Brogollia Attorneys which advertised on national television and I wondered at the time how they could afford to do so. In a recent award by the Fund, one of their clients was paid R1.7 million for a minor injury worth only R20,000. Not a bad legal fee if the lawyers got say 25% of the claim. Many rumours abound about kickbacks to Fund officials by law firms. No aspect of life is unaffected by corruption. In this past financial year, the Fund operated at a net loss of R322 billion – ludicrous considering the massive inflow of funds via a fuel levy on every litre sold. In a landmark court decision in 2021, the Supreme Court of Appeal sided with the government and ordered the Court Sheriffs not to proceed with the attachment and sale in execution of the Fund's assets including its bank accounts, for non-payment of claims in terms of other lower court judgments. The SCA cited the avoidance of a *constitutional crisis* as its main consideration. So much for judicial independence. The public is now unprotected if injured in road accidents, while attorneys who specialised in road accident claims are now toothless in respect of their next crust of bread.

A lady black attorney was favoured with executorship appointments by an official of the Master of the High Court whenever no executor had been nominated in a Will, earning a 3.5% executor's fee on the gross assets in each estate he handled.

125

Gwede Mantashe's son is a major player in the country's only paid TV satellite supplier DSTV, which costs nearly double the most expensive equivalent in the UK. Another favoured BEE cadre.

It looks like even the SA Revenue Services (SARS) is involved in shenanigans. Nationally, employees were told that if they earned below a certain threshold and only submitted their PAYE and medical forms, they would not have to submit a tax return and the computer system would simply calculate any tax refund due and credit their bank accounts. One taxpayer was recently refunded R3,400 and when her accountant did a proper calculation it was found this should have been R18,000. One wonders who would have profited, the government or a corrupt official, were it not for the accountant? A similar thing happened to my wife years ago after she packed up work due to her disability but unfortunately, she never got to the bottom of it despite employing an accountant to tackle SARS.

One of the SOEs, the Post Office has just reported a quarterly loss of R429 million, with a combined loss for the year of just under R2 billion. Bailouts from the ANC to the Post Office to date amount to some R8 billion. Some post offices have been forced to close due to being unable to pay the rent.

In the 2021/22 Budget, the finance minister revealed the education budget is to be cut by R120 billion and the police budget by R80 billion – another major deterioration in public services.

The three major international rating agencies have in 2021 all further downgraded SA's credit rating. Moody's rating is now Ba2, which is two notches below junk status and Fitch's rating is three notches below junk status.

The lockdowns in SA have all but destroyed tourism on which the country depended for foreign exchange and fiscal revenue, previously worth R125 Billion a year and employing 800,000 people. Some claim this is a ploy by the ANC for its cadres to acquire premium holiday properties at fire-sale prices.

SA had plenty of time in 2020 but the ANC was too busy plundering the IMF loan to order Covid vaccines. Ramaphosa is now calling them *apartheid vaccines*.

At the current rate, it will take 20 years to vaccinate the population.

Within Ramaphosa's presidential department, new employees have been appointed without copies of certificates or any proof of their supposed qualifications.

The police services failed to pay for forensic services rendered and the providers have since December 2020 refused to do any further DNA or forensic tests, bringing rape cases among others to a standstill. At last count, the backlog of DNA tests totalled 270,000. It was revealed in 2021 that SA's Forensics Department has collapsed. It is no longer able to do DNA tests due to the department's non-payment of amounts owing to service providers. There are now a reported 170,000 cases of rape, murder and child abuse going unprosecuted as a result. Statistically, 80% of all murder cases in SA are closed as unsolved.

Zwelini Mkhize, Minister of Health, recently awarded a Covid contract for R82 million to a company whose managing director is employed as a petrol pump attendant at a service station in Durban. Any investigation is unlikely.

SA's standing in the sporting world has all but collapsed mainly as a result of racial quotas taking preference over abilities. Conspicuously, many top SA sportsmen and women have moved overseas to obtain professional sporting contracts.

The latest *solution* to SA's electricity crisis is to park eight power ships from Turkey at an annual cost of R20 billion to make up the supply shortfall. However, the plan is being stalled because Transnet, the Harbour Authority has not yet permitted these ships to be docked in the harbours for 20 years – not to mention the obvious lack of affordability of the government.

The ANC owes SARS over R80 million for unpaid PAYE, taxes deducted from its employees' salaries but not paid over, an offence that would land any other employer in prison.

The latest SA youth (ages 15 – 24) unemployment rates reveal 74.7% are jobless. Surely a recipe for disaster?

[Source: The Times, 7 June 2021, the article reads: The first generation of South Africans to have lived free of apartheid are trapped in the country's worst ever youth unemployment. Known as the "born frees", the cohort that have only known democratic rule is confronting an unemployment rate of 74.7 per cent. Statistics SA, which published the figures from the last quarter of last year, counted those aged between 15 and 24 in its youth jobless rate. Data gathered from 200 countries for The Global Economy website puts SA at the top for highest number of unemployed youth.].

South Africa has the highest number of unemployed youth among 200 countries studied by The Global Economy
Siphiwe Sibeko/Reuters Acknowleged

The Finale

For the reasons above, I believe that the ANC will continue to rule for many years to come. Democracy only works if the losers accept defeat in free and fair elections. This will not happen, whether by hook or crook the ANC will cling to power. There has been some talk of the Western Cape seceding from the rest of the country but the ANC will never countenance such a move. And with the ANC in control of the military and police forces, this is very unlikely. A recent report suggested that the army employed 73,000 people but of this number only 3,000 are fighting fit.

A third scenario is an apparent threat from the terrorist organisation Al Shabab which is gaining a foothold in Mozambique and moving southwards. Given the state of the SA forces, it should not meet too much resistance if its ultimate plan is to plunder the resources of a country like SA.

The further threat to the country as we know it is the colonisation by the Chinese who have acquired businesses in recent times and set up a huge motor manufacturing plant in PE. We have seen that China has given the government loans and is being repaid by supplying coal to China. A recent video showed huge coal trucks lined up for a couple of kilometres, waiting to access Richard's Bay Harbour, export destination China. One can only guess what is happening with other minerals. It is reported that Mandarin is being taught in more than 50 schools across SA; with socialism already well-entrenched, SA on its way to becoming a communist state.

Finally, there is the real threat of violence breaking out between the two factions within the ANC, the one led by Zuma who controls KZN with his ally, Ace Magashule who controls a large support base in the Free State, on the one hand, and the remainder of the ANC under Ramaphosa on the other. If President Ramaphosa fails to unify the ruling party, who knows what might happen, especially as Zuma and Magashule will not allow themselves to be singled out as *scapegoats* while the rest of the ANC elite enjoy the fruits of their rampant corruption.

There is the odd ray of sunshine. If Herman Mashaba and his newly established Action SA Party can carry out the reforms he has promised if elected, who knows, perhaps SA will also experience (for Mashaba) a French President Macron-style landslide victory?

Even if the chances are as great as being struck by lightning.

As this book goes to publication, the chickens are coming home to roost, with a wave of rioting, looting and destruction across KZN and Gauteng, accompanied by many individual casualties and deaths. The first world war erupted following the assassination of a Duke; in the case of SA, the imprisonment of Jacob Zuma struck the match that lit the powder keg. Everything portrayed in this book is evidenced by events now taking place.

Many people are painting different scenarios, but the underlying inescapable truth is that:

- hungry people are angry people (despite scenes of *fat cats* and policemen being among the looters);
- no one knows what political agenda is behind all of this, but certainly the retention of power by the ANC remains paramount for the majority, although there are definite factions within the ANC which might well lead to a tribal war, Zulus versus the rest;
- after six days of unbridled looting, Ramaphosa finally issued a statement saying the looting was planned and that he will go after the perpetrators, while he turns a blind eye to the rape and pillaging of the country by the ANC;
- Ramaphosa further observed that *the democracy of South Africa is being undermined,* again seemingly blind to the ANC having reduced democracy to virtual non-existence;
- the figures are that this mass-scale wave of violence has cost the country another 100,000 jobs and further losses of at least R50 billion. Thousands of businesses and vehicles have been destroyed and many are now starving and suffering due to food, fuel and medicine shortages, and the closing down of road transportation;
- when the looting and burning took place, the government was unable or unwilling to take action early on;

- due to the mismanagement and corruption, the police were short of ammunition to deal with the crowds of looters, and the security industry had to provide arms and assistance to the police;
- one positive from all this was citizens banding together to protect themselves and their properties, with the Police Chief promising to fast-track gun licences (in the face of recent legislation to disarm ordinary citizens) – although if a full-scale *revolution* takes place, or civil war erupts, it is doubtful the hopelessly outnumbered ordinary citizens would prevail.

The open questions remain, how will SA ever get rid of the ANC and, if this should ever happen, what party/militia will replace it? SA has indeed become *just another African country*.

Any way you look at it, the future for SA is indeed bleak and thank goodness I can watch these events unfold from afar. The dictionary defines a **kakistocracy** (kakɪˈstɒkrəsi/noun) as *government by the least suitable or competent citizens of a state.*

Chapter 17

Making a Move – the Solution?

Make the move? For many SA-born persons, this may not seem an option. However, lots of people who thought they cannot *escape to pastures greener* have discovered that, actually, they can. One of the hardest things to do during one's lifetime, particularly when you are well-established in terms of business, lifestyle, your circle of friends and family, is to uproot yourself and move to another country. Let us not be mistaken, this takes courage. Over the years I have witnessed many people who saw the writing on the wall emigrate from SA. Some have returned after making a go of things in their new surroundings, but they are in the extreme minority. I have always said that if you are serious about making the move you have to allow at least 5 years at your chosen destination before rethinking your decision.

In my case I previously stated that after my fact-finding mission in 1977, I decided SA was where I wanted to work and live. Having been there through all the stages of SA's development from 1952 to 2019, I have no particular regrets regarding that decision. We had a good standard of living, enjoyed the fruits of our labour and I feel certain we made a meaningful contribution to all things SA. The hardest part in relocating is the family and friends you leave behind. In our case as I have said, most of our family were already in the UK which made it a whole lot easier for us. After all, one can visit SA as often as time and finances allow. Earning a "hard currency" such as Sterling, also makes this easier.

When we left SA in October 2019, I told everyone that I was going for 3 to 6 months to see how things panned out and within a few months of our arrival in England, the coronavirus pandemic hit the world, and changed everything. Not only were we effectively stranded in the UK but the resultant extra time gave us a chance to sort out our lives here and adapt to a new way of life. And a rather different culture to what we expected, with SA having once been a British colony; there is a significant difference in cultures.

There are many things which cause people to make up their minds to emigrate but, in a nutshell set out below are most, if not all the reasons for South Africans who are able to do so, to "make the move".

If you can dodge the following in South Africa:

- Crime in all its forms;
- Being unemployed and having no income;
- Substandard health care;
- The lack of a decent education for your children;
- The lack of electricity;
- The lack of decent drinking water;
- The lack of proper policing
- The lawlessness and potholes on the roads and not being a statistic of the high unacceptable accident rate
- Paying exorbitant taxes for which you get very little in return after a a large portion has been stolen every year
- Having your land / investments expropriated or confiscated
- Being subjected to numerous labour laws which make it impossible to do business profitably

– you are then one of the *Remainers* in SA – but know this, the one thing you will not be able to dodge is hyperinflation which is gaining momentum and will wipe out all your pension, retirement plans and investments.

From my perspective the only dodgy thing about the UK is the winter weather which at its worst is still bearable. When it comes to the oft-mentioned average 300 days a year of rain, we often experience four seasons in a day. Much of the rain falls at night, or during the day it may rain for say twenty minutes and then the sun comes out for the rest of the day. Since our 2019 arrival in the UK, I have only used an umbrella three or four times. English gardens are famous throughout the world. Everything grows easily and the countryside is lush and green, thanks to the regular rainfall.

South Africans who leave SA cite violent crime and lack of employment (thanks to affirmative action aka BEE) as the two main reasons for doing so. After all, if you fear for your safety and cannot earn a decent living, there have to be greener pastures elsewhere.

In our case, apart from the issue of crime and the general lack of safety and policing, the remaining pointers for us were that our children and grandchildren were mostly already living in the UK, and the fear that should hyperinflation set in there would be no safety net to fall back on – certainly, the ANC cannot even look after what it terms its *own people*. In addition, as we hit old age perhaps the paramount reason is the UK's guaranteed world-class healthcare *on the house* – that's how a government spends tax payers' money wisely!

People in the younger generations have more serious considerations to take into account, including worrying about their and their children's future, where they will likely be locked out of the economic system and even if they do have entrepreneurial business skills, will they be happy following all the labour policies, red tape and eventually giving up a large percentage of their profits, if not the business itself, to BEE?

Parents who have young children should worry about their long-term future and not just sit on the fence waiting to see how things pan out. You do not see the day-to-day regression in SA but if you can make a move, you should consider things carefully. After all, one day when SA has a proper government in place it will need all the skills and help it can get for rebuilding the country. A return to the fold for you at that point would be welcomed with open arms. On the other hand, if the ANC stays in power for generations to come *a la* Mugabe-style it will just not be worth living in SA for the majority of people.

Change will eventually come but the questions are when and how?

As things stand it won't be an orderly transition. Our experience living in a first-world country has opened our eyes, where taxes are spent as they should be, on uplifting the citizens of the country and if there is the smallest hint of corruption it is dealt with harshly. In return for proper governance, you are mostly safe from crime, have first-world healthcare, great public transport systems, no worries about lack of water or electricity, low inflation rate, decent infrastructure, all of which are examples of how things should work. And of course, proper democracy and accountability. Many SA people I know are very comfortable living in a *bubble*, but the clock ticks every day, and it reminds me of the clock on the wall of the Port Alfred Golf Club that goes backwards.

It was a revelation to discover that in the UK, people can walk in safety late at night, or alone in the forests, or on the beaches. Couples fall asleep on park lawns, their mobile phones and handbags next to them. Certainly, there is crime in every country, but your chances of becoming a crime statistic in the UK are so many times lower than in SA. More so when it comes to violent crime. CCTV is ubiquitous and if the police are determined to catch a culprit they will invariably do so.

Many South Africans say, "But SA is so beautiful" ... Let me comment that the UK is equally stunning in its beauty, clean and crystal-clear river waters, all the verdant shades of green, manicured parks and gardens, forests, coastline and beaches, and country roads lined by hedgerows.

There is no excuse if you know you need to get yourself and your family to a safer place to live. Is that not, after all, our responsibility (since the ANC has clearly abrogated in this regard – just ask the farmers)? Yes, you may say, that's easy if you have a British passport. It may be easier but, as the old saying goes, *Where there's a Will, there's a Relative.*

If you have certain minimum capital amounts, you can enter the UK as an entrepreneur. There are special work permits and employers

135

(in a country where the unemployment rate is below 5%, with Covid, up from 2% pre-Covid) are prepared to sponsor employees from SA who have special skills, e.g. IT, coding, and many other fields.

The UK Start-up visa offers a wonderful opportunity for persons who want to set up a new and innovative business in the UK. This immigration route will allow the successful applicant to come to the UK for two years. You can read more here: https://bic-immigration.com/uk-immigration/start-up-visa/.
I strongly recommend a consultation with Breytenbachs Immigration Consultants. We used them for my wife's spousal visa and cannot recommend Breytenbachs highly enough. They have offices in SA and the UK. There are also the UK Intra-Company Transfer Visa, the UK Skilled Worker Visa, the Health and Care Worker Visa, the UK Student Visa, and the UK Creative and Sporting Visa.

It is worthwhile checking your options on Google.

If you have a business in SA, America offers an L1 visa, whereby you are virtually guaranteed a 2-year residency permit for yourself *and* your dependants, if you open a branch of your SA business there, provided you motivate this by adding that you foresee employing Americans within a couple of years of launching there. At the end of the 2 years, you and your family with you will qualify for Green Cards.

New Zealand will grab anyone able to work with their hands. If you are an artisan, according to actual experiences of persons I know, you can arrive in NZ on a tourist visa, no cash, no assets, obtain a job there, and your new boss will arrange your work visa for you. After a time, you qualify for permanent residence status. Then NZ citizenship will follow. If Australia is your end-goal, NZ provides the perfect stepping stone for next getting into Australia.

Canada welcomes skilled people with open arms, and minimum fuss.

About the Author:

Christopher R Cornish was born in London shortly after World War II and raised in South Africa, to where his parents emigrated, given the hardships at the time and opportunities which opened up in developing Commonwealth countries. He witnessed the evils of the apartheid era and the events which unfolded in the *New South Africa* post-1994, including the handover of power to the former liberation movement, the ANC, and subsequent deterioration into just another third world African country – where those in power are only in it for personal gain. He and his wife decided in 2019 that South Africa was no longer the place to see out their days, and returned to his roots in England.

If you enjoyed reading this book, please leave a kind review on Amazon.

Printed in Great Britain
by Amazon

13882415R00091